HOUGHTON MIFFLIN

English

Texas Edition

Authors
Robert Rueda
Tina Saldivar
Lynne Shapiro
Shane Templeton
C. Ann Terry
Catherine Valentino
Shelby A. Wolf

Consultants
Jeanneine P. Jones
Monette Coleman McIver
Rojulene Norris

 HOUGHTON MIFFLIN   BOSTON • MORRIS PLAINS, NJ

California • Colorado • Georgia • Illinois • New Jersey • Texas

Acknowledgments

For each of the selections listed below, grateful acknowledgment is made for permission to excerpt and/or reprint original or copyrighted material as follows:

Published Models

From "Gloria Who Might Be My Best Friend" from THE STORIES JULIAN TELLS by Ann Cameron. Copyright ©1981 by Ann Cameron. Cover illustration copyright ©1981 by Ann Strugnell. Reprinted by permission of Random House Children's Books, a division of Random House, Inc.

From HIDE AND SEEK FOG by Alvin Tresselt, illustrated by Roger Duvoisin. Copyright ©1965 by Lothrop, Lee & Shepard Co., Inc. Used by permission of HarperCollins Publishers.

From "How to Make a Bag of Rain" from YOUR BIG BACKYARD Magazine, June 1999 issue, a publication of the National Wildlife Federation. Copyright ©1999 by National Wildlife Federation. Reprinted by permission of National Wildlife Federation.

"My Life in the Country" by Tomie dePaola. Copyright ©2001 by Tomie dePaola. Reprinted by permission of the author.

THE WOLF'S CHICKEN STEW by Keiko Kasza. Copyright ©1987 by Keiko Kasza. Reprinted by permission of Putnam & Grosset Group, a division of Penguin Putnam Inc.

Poetry

"Commas" from BING BANG BOING by Douglas Florian. Copyright ©1994 by Douglas Florian. Reprinted with permission of Harcourt, Inc.

"Fishes' Evening Song" from WHISPERING AND OTHER THINGS by Dahlov Ipcar. Copyright ©1967 by Dahlov Ipcar. Published by Alfred A. Knopf, Inc. Reprinted by permission of McIntosh and Otis, Inc.

Acknowledgments are continued at the back of the book following the last page of the Index.

ISBN: 0-618-05488-X

456789-VH-06 05 04 03 02 01

TABLE OF CONTENTS

Tools and Tips H2

Listening, Speaking, and Viewing

Every day you listen, speak, and view things. What do you think these people are listening to, saying, or viewing?

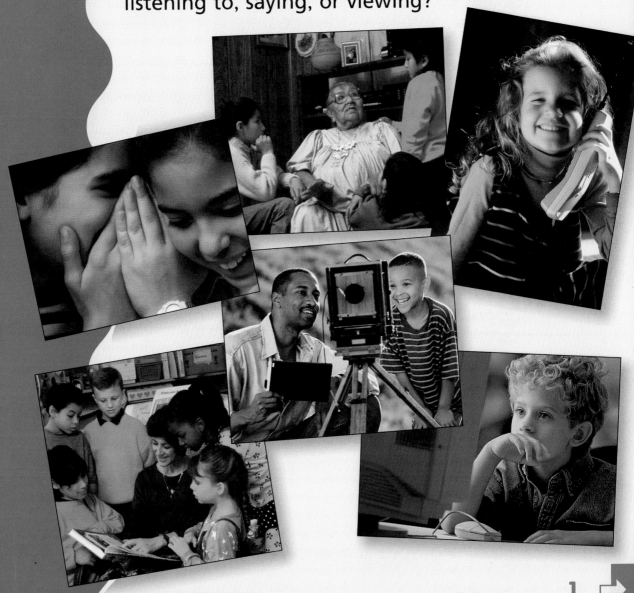

Learning Together

Each one of you is special. You share "pieces of yourself" with others when you **speak**. You learn from others when you **listen** or **view**.

Think and Discuss

These children made posters about why people listen, speak, and view. Read their posters.

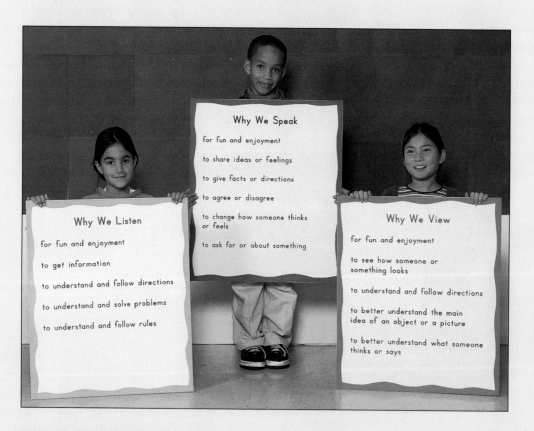

Why We Speak

for fun and enjoyment

to share ideas or feelings

to give facts or directions

to agree or disagree

to change how someone thinks or feels

to ask for or about something

Why We Listen

for fun and enjoyment

to get information

to understand and follow directions

to understand and solve problems

to understand and follow rules

Why We View

for fun and enjoyment

to see how someone or something looks

to understand and follow directions

to better understand the main idea of an object or a picture

to better understand what someone thinks or says

Try It Together

Make a class list of times and places that you have used listening, speaking, and viewing.

Being a Good Listener

Every day you hear sounds, music, and words. Read how listening is more than just hearing!

Think and Discuss

Read the Listening Tips. Which tips are these children following?

Listening Tips

- Look at the speaker.
- Pay attention.
- Think about what the speaker is reading or saying.
- Ask questions if you do not understand.

Try It Together

Listen as your teacher reads a story aloud.
Then answer the questions.

Being a Good Speaker

When you speak, you want people to hear and think about what you say.

When you speak to friends, you might use different words and sentences than you would use if you were speaking to an adult.

Think and Discuss

Read the Speaking Tips. Which tip is this child following?

Speaking Tips

- Think about what you will say.
- Speak clearly and loudly enough for your audience.
- Use words and sentences that "fit" your listeners.
- Look at your listeners.

Try It Together

Draw a picture of an animal. Think of a short story about it. Tell it to your classmates as if you are talking to friends. Then tell it again as if you are talking to adults.

Having a Conversation

A conversation is a friendly talk. You can talk about many different things.

In a conversation, take turns listening and speaking. Ask or answer questions, share ideas, or tell how you feel.

Think and Discuss

In what ways are these children being good listeners and speakers?

Try It Together

With a group, have a conversation about what each of you did yesterday after school.

Having a Discussion

A discussion is a talk in which people share their ideas on one main topic. To have a good discussion, follow these tips.

Discussion Tips

- Share your ideas. They are important!
- Take turns. Wait for others to finish speaking before you begin.
- Speak clearly and loudly enough for everyone to hear.
- Keep to the topic.
- Let others share their ideas. Don't do all the talking.
- Look at the person speaking.
- If you do not agree with someone, say so politely.
- Think about what each person says. Ask questions if you do not understand.

Think and Discuss

Look at the photo on the next page. The children are discussing a class picnic! Which Discussion Tips are they following?

Try It Together

With a group, have a discussion about places to go on a class field trip.

Being a Good Viewer

All day long you see pictures and objects. Read how viewing is more than just seeing!

Think and Discuss

Read the Viewing Tips. Which tips are these children following?

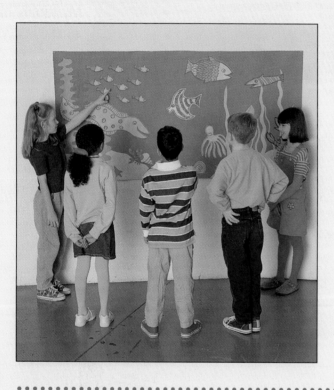

Viewing Tips

- First, look at the whole picture or object.
- Then take a longer, closer look at each part.
- Ask yourself questions.
- Think about the message, main idea, or theme.

Try It Together

View a picture from a magazine. Tell a classmate exactly what you see. Then tell how the picture makes you feel or explain the message you get from the picture.

Viewing: Looking and Thinking

Pictures help you understand what you read. News videos help you understand what you hear. Posters, signs, and displays send messages.

Think and Discuss

How are the parts of this display alike? How are they different? Think about what you already know about its main idea. What message do you think it sends?

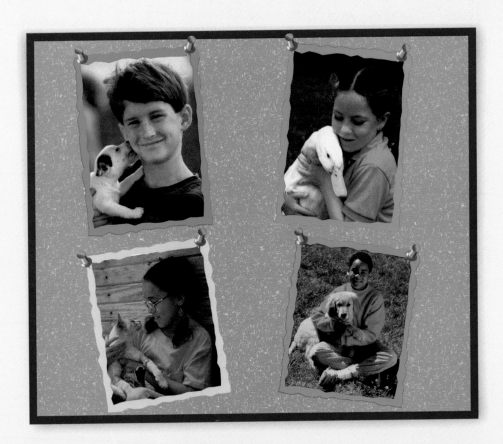

Viewing continued

Lynn learned about something that she wanted to share with her classmates. She made a poster with pictures to help her classmates understand it.

Try It Together

With a classmate, view Lynn's poster. What is the same in each picture? What is different? What is the main idea of the poster? How do Lynn's pictures help her classmates understand what she wrote?

The Writing Process

Every day children and adults write at home, in school, at work, and at play! Look at these pictures. What do you think these people are writing?

The Writing Process

Hi! I'm W.R. the Writing Star. I'm going to help you learn to write, using **the Writing Process.** Just take a look!

1 PREWRITING

First, I plan my writing.

police officer

our room

last week

visited

2 DRAFTING

Next, I write a draft.

A police officer visited our room last week

3 Then I make my writing better.

Officer Brown
^A police officer
                    classroom
visited our ^room& last

week^ to talk about safety

Next, I check and fix my writing.

Officer Brown
A police officer
^
              classroom
visited our ^room& last

week^ to talk about safety.

4

Finally, I copy my writing neatly and share it.

5

Officer Brown visited

our classroom last week

to talk about safety.

Prewriting

Choosing a Topic for a Class Story

The children in Mr. Ortiz's class wanted to let their families know about something interesting they had done. They began by listing their topic ideas.

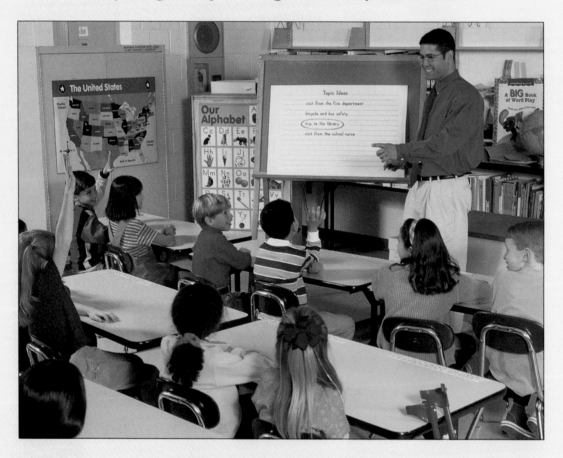

They discussed the topics and chose to write about their trip to the library.

Learning from a Model

Topic Ideas

visit from the fire department

bicycle and bus safety

(trip to the library)

visit from the school nurse

▶ **Choose Your Topic**

❶ **Write** something that your class has done that you would like to write about.

❷ **Make** a class list of everyone's ideas. Discuss the ideas with your class.

❸ **Choose** one idea to write about as a whole class.

❹ **Copy** and complete these sentences. Name your topic and audience.

We will write about _____.

_____ will read or hear our story.

> Answer these questions to help you choose an idea.
> • Would we like to write about this?
> • Do we remember enough about it?
> • Will a reader be interested?

Getting Started: The Writing Process

Prewriting continued

Exploring a Topic for a Class Story

The children thought about their trip to the library. Then they used a word web to explore their topic.

Learning from a Model

story time

librarian

Mrs. Brown   trip to library

fun place   library cards
to visit

checked out books

▶ **Explore Your Class Story Topic**

1 **Explore** your topic with your class.

2 **Tell** your teacher important details that should be included in your story. Your teacher will record your details in a word web.

Organizing Details for a Class Story

The children looked at their word web. Then they told Mr. Ortiz what happened on their trip in the order that it happened. He wrote the details in a Sequence Chart.

Sequence Chart
First met the librarian—Mrs. Brown
Next got library cards checked out books
Last story time with Mrs. Brown

▶ **Organize Your Details**

1 **Discuss** your topic and details from your word web.

2 **Help** your teacher make a Sequence Chart.

Drafting

Drafting a Class Story

Mr. Ortiz wrote the working draft of the class story, as the children told him what to write. Mr. Ortiz indented his paragraph and wrote a topic sentence. He skipped lines as he wrote so that the class could make changes later.

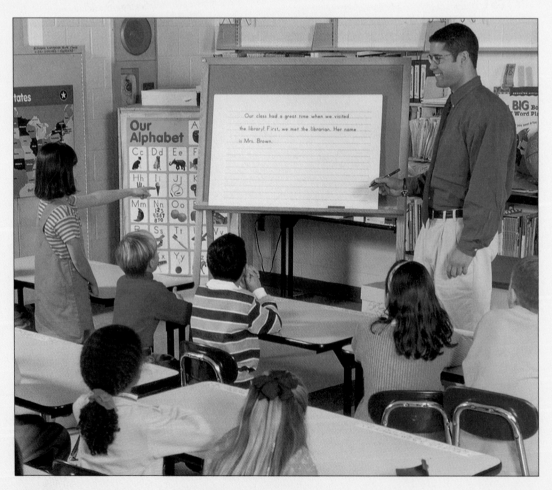

Learning from a Model

Our class had a great time when we visited the library! First, we met the librarian. Her name is Mrs. Brown. Next, she gave each of us a library card. ~~We read~~ Then we checked out books. ~~Finally~~ Before we left, Mrs. Brown read us a story. Our library is a fun place to visit.

▶ Draft Your Class Story

> The topic sentence tells the main idea of your story.

1. **Write** a topic sentence that makes a good beginning for your class story.

2. **Share** your sentence. As a class, choose one topic sentence to begin your class story.

3. **Use** the details in your Sequence Chart to tell your story to your teacher. Your teacher will write the working draft. You can fix mistakes and make changes later.

Revising

Revising a Class Story

The children read their working draft aloud. They talked about how to make it clearer and more interesting for their families. Then the class decided on some changes to make. Mr. Ortiz made the changes to the working draft.

Learning from a Model

Our class had a great time when we visited the library! First, we met the librarian. Her name is Mrs. Brown. Next, she gave each of us a library card. ~~We read~~ Then we ∧used the card to checked out books. ~~Finally~~ Before we left, Mrs. Brown read us a story.∧ It was called Amos and Boris. Our library is a fun place to visit.

▶ **Revise Your Class Story**

1 **Read** your class story aloud.

2 **Write** two things that you would like to change to make the story better.

3 **Talk** with your class about changes you think would make the story better. Together, decide which changes to make.

4 **Help** your teacher revise your class story.

> When you revise, think about your audience. Add details to help them picture what happened.

Proofreading

Proofreading a Class Story

Each child in Mr. Ortiz's class copied the revised class story. Then the children used proofreading marks to fix mistakes. Look at Nita's proofread story.

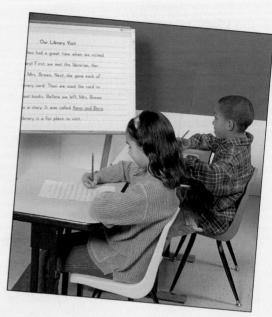

Learning from a Model

Our class had a great time when we

visited the library! First, we met the librarian.

Her name is Mrs. brown. Next, she gave each

of us a library card. Then we used the card to

check out ~~boks~~ books. Before we left, Mrs. Brown

read us a story. It was called Amos and Boris.

Our library is a fun place to visit.

Proofread Your Class Story

1 **Write** your own copy of your class story.

2 **Proofread** your class story. Use the Proofreading Checklist and Proofreading Marks.

Proofreading Checklist

- Each sentence begins with a capital letter.

- Each sentence ends with the correct mark.

- Each word is spelled correctly.

Point to each word as you proofread.

Proofreading Marks

∧ Add	≡ Capital letter
⌒ Delete	/ Small letter
¶ Indent for new paragraph	

3 **Use** a class dictionary to check the spellings of words.

📖 See the Spelling Guide on page H40.

Publishing

Publishing a Class Story

Mr. Ortiz's class thought of a good way to publish the class story for their families. Mr. Ortiz made a neat final copy, and the children drew pictures to go with it. They displayed them for Parents Night.

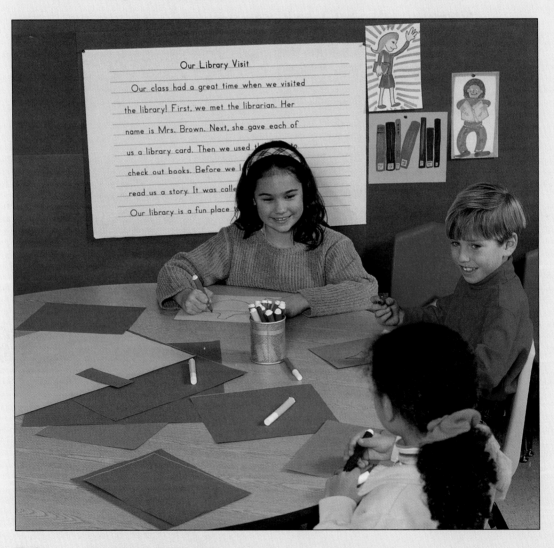

Our Library Visit

Our class had a great time when we visited the library! First, we met the librarian. Her name is Mrs. Brown. Next, she gave each of us a library card. Then we used th... to check out books. Before we l... read us a story. It was calle... Our library is a fun place t...

▶ Publish Your Class Story

1 Talk with your class about different ways to share your story.

2 Choose a special way to share your class story with your audience.

3 Make a neat final copy of your class story. Be sure you wrote your letters correctly and used good spacing.

4 Write an interesting title. Be sure to begin the first, last, and each important word with a capital letter.

▶ Reflect

Together, talk about these questions.

- What was easy about writing this class story?
- What was hard?
- What did you learn about the writing process?

The Sentence

Snow fell today. The polar bears play.

1 What Is a Sentence?

Who did something? What did that person or animal do?

Mr. Putter cheered. Tabby purred and hiccuped.

—from Mr. Putter and Tabby Fly the Plane, by Cynthia Rylant

A **sentence** tells what someone or something did or does. Who played? What do the blocks do?

The boy played. **The blocks fall.**

Try It Out

Speak Up Match the groups of words to say sentences about the picture.

1. A balloon   rings.
2. The train   popped.
3. The bell   goes fast.

Write It Now write the sentences.

Example The girl   ran.

                    smiled.

         The girl smiled.

Match the words in Box **A** with the words in Box **B** to make sentences. Then write the sentences.

Example The boy flies. The boy plays.
                               plays.

A	**B**
1. The ball	walked.
2. The plane	floats.
3. The robot	rolled.
4. The boat	flies.

5–6. Match the groups of words to make sentences. Copy the ad title. Write the sentences to finish the ad.

- The horns   ring.
- The bells   toot.

Buy These Noisy Toys!

Writing Wrap-Up WRITING • THINKING • LISTENING • SPEAKING

DESCRIBING

Write Sentences

Write sentences that tell about a toy. Draw a picture of it. Then read your sentences aloud. Have classmates tell what the toy can do or what you do with the toy.

2 Naming Part

One-Minute Warm-Up

Think of a person or animal that you could find at the circus. Act out something it does. Have a classmate name the person or animal.

The **naming part** of a sentence tells who or what did or does something. Read the sentences. Who went to the circus? What jumps through a hoop?

Jason went to the circus.

A dog jumps through a hoop.

Try It Out

Speak Up Say a naming part from the Word Box to begin each sentence about the picture.

A bear	A girl	The clown

1. _____ holds the hoop.

2. _____ stood on a horse.

Write It Now write each sentence. Draw a line under the naming part.

Example _____ sat on a ball.

A bear sat on a ball.

Choose a naming part from the Word Box to begin each sentence. Write the sentences.

Example _____ clap. Children clap.

Children
Dogs
Clowns

1. _____ juggle.   **2.** _____ bark.

3–6. Copy the circus poster. Write a naming part from the Word Box to begin each sentence.

Horses	Lions	Clowns	A man	A band

Example _____ **make us laugh.** Clowns make us laugh.

Come to the Circus!

_____ roar.   _____ plays music.

_____ prance.   _____ sells balloons.

Writing Wrap-Up

WRITING • THINKING • LISTENING • SPEAKING

DESCRIBING

Write Circus Poster Sentences

Make your own circus poster. Tell what people and animals do at a circus. Add pictures. Show your poster and read the sentences. Have a classmate say the naming part of each sentence.

3 Action Part

Act out something you can or like to do. Have classmates guess the action you are doing.

The **action part** of a sentence tells what the naming part did or does. Tell what Ken did or does.

Ken **followed the signs**.   Ken **slides**.

Try It Out

Speak Up Say an action part from the Word Box to finish each sentence.

showed what to do	climbed a pole
walked on a log	watched

1. Ken _____.

2. Anna _____.

3. A chipmunk _____.

Write It Now write the sentences.

Example The signs _____.

The signs showed what to do.

Choose an action part from the Word Box
to finish each sentence. Write the sentences.

| writes books | makes bread | makes us well |

Example A baker_____. A baker makes bread.

1. A doctor _____.

2. An author _____.

3–4. Choose an action part from the Word Box to finish
each sentence on Rosa's list. Write the title and sentences.

| grows food | flies a jet | fixes teeth |

Example A dentist _____. A dentist fixes teeth.

Jobs People Do

A pilot _____.
A farmer _____.

Writing Wrap-Up

Write a List

Write three sentences about jobs people do in your school or
class. Read your sentences. Have a classmate name the action
parts. Discuss if you would like to do these jobs.

4 Is It a Sentence?

Say the naming part and the action part in each sentence.

Father kissed her again. Mother kissed her again.
They closed the door.

—from Bedtime for Frances, by Russell Hoban

A complete sentence has a **naming part** and an **action part**. Read this sentence. Say the naming part. Say the action part.

A big frog jumps off a rock.

Try It Out

Speak Up Which two word groups are complete sentences? Read them aloud and tell why.

1. Sleeps on a log.

2. Fish swim in the water.

3. Three birds sing.

4. The green frog.

Write It Now write the two complete sentences.

Example Floats on the pond. A lily pad floats.
　　　　　A lily pad floats.

Read and copy each word group. Write **yes** after each complete sentence. Write **no** after the other word groups.

Example The seeds open. yes

1. Plants grow.

2. Floats away.

3. Deep water.

4. It falls down.

5–6. Read each word group. Write the two complete sentences to make a sign like the one below.

Example Ducks live here. Ducks live here.
A big lake.

• Children swim here.

• Swims and runs.

• Little children and dogs.

• All boats stay out.

Warning!

Writing Wrap-Up

Write Sentences for a Sign

Write two complete sentences to make a sign for your bedroom door. Read them to a classmate. Have the classmate say each naming part and action part.

Writing Complete Sentences ⭐

Completing Sentences Write complete sentences. Each one must have a **naming part** and an **action part**.

> **Monkeys play in the jungle.**

Try It Out

Speak Up Look at each picture and the word group under it. Add a naming part or an action part to the word group to say a complete sentence about the picture.

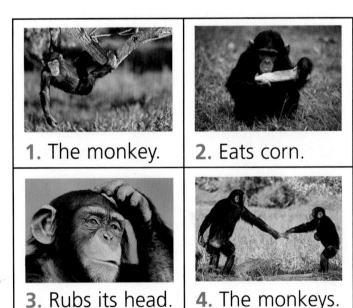

1. The monkey.

2. Eats corn.

3. Rubs its head.

4. The monkeys.

Write It 1–4. Now write the four complete sentences. Begin and end them correctly.

Example That monkey. That monkey jumps.

Revising Strategies continued

Apply It

1–2. Read this part of a journal entry. Copy one word group that is not a sentence. Add a naming part or an action part to that word group to write a complete sentence.

Example The pandas.

The pandas play.

Revising

On Saturday, my family visited the new zoo in our town. We saw lots of animals there. A panda and its sister. I really liked the pandas.

3–6. Read the rest of the entry. Copy two word groups that are not sentences. Add a naming part or an action part to each word group to write two complete sentences.

Revising

On the way home, we stopped for lunch. My sister and I ate salad and pizza. Tasted good. Later, we watched a video about pandas. The cute pandas.

36   Writing Complete Sentences

5 Telling Sentences

Read these sentences. What place do they tell about? Tell what you know about that place.

Life on the farm wasn't always this way. Everything changed just last Saturday.

—from <u>Mrs. Brown Went to Town</u>, by Wong Herbert Yee

A **telling sentence** tells something. It begins with a **capital letter**. It ends with a **period**.

Some animals live on farms**.**

Horses live there**.**

Try It Out

Speak Up Tell how to make each sentence correct.

1. the sheep are in a pen.

2. Pigs roll in the mud

3. cows eat grass

Write It Now write the sentences correctly.

Example chickens lay eggs

Chickens lay eggs.

Write each sentence correctly.

Example the sun shines

The sun shines.

1. It is hot   **2.** the cat naps

3–6. Proofread this post card. Find four mistakes with capital letters and periods. Write the message correctly.

Example we swam in the pond

We swam in the pond.

Proofreading

Dear Mom and Dad,

we fed the chickens
We rode the horses
the farm is very busy.

Tim and Pam

Mr. and Mrs. Adams
7 Baker Street
Tampa, Florida 33605

Writing Wrap-Up   WRITING • THINKING • LISTENING • SPEAKING

DESCRIBING

Write a Post Card Message
Write and draw about a place. Read your sentences to a classmate. Together, check for capital letters and periods.

6 Questions

Look at the picture. What is the squirrel looking at? What might it be thinking? Say a sentence that the squirrel might ask if it could talk.

A **question** is a sentence that asks something. A question begins with a **capital letter** and ends with a **question mark**.

What is your name**?**

Do you like trees**?**

Try It Out

Speak Up Tell how to make each question correct.

1. will it eat seeds?

2. is the squirrel red

3. Where does it live

Write It Now write the questions correctly.

Example did it find acorns

Did it find acorns?

Write the correct question in each pair.

Example what is that in the sky. What is that in the sky?
What is that in the sky?

1. Is the moon up there?
is the moon up there?

3. Is that a rocket?
Is that a rocket

2. Do you see the stars
Do you see the stars?

4. where is it going?
Where is it going?

5–8. Proofread Jan's science questions. Find four mistakes with capital letters and end marks. Write each question correctly.

Example what do I want to know.
What do I want to know?

Proofreading

how big are rockets?

Are all rockets the same size

Can a rocket reach Mars?

where are rockets built

Writing Wrap-Up

WRITING • THINKING • LISTENING • SPEAKING

INFORMING

Write Questions

Write three questions that you can answer correctly. Read your questions to classmates. Have them try to answer the questions.

For Extra Practice, see page 58.

7 Which Kind of Sentence?

Look at the picture below. Ask questions about it. Invite classmates to answer with telling sentences.

A sentence can ask a question or tell something. A **question** ends with a question mark. A **telling sentence** ends with a period. Read the question. Then read the telling sentence that answers it.

What is in the balloon?

Pets are in the balloon.

Try It Out

Speak Up Read each sentence and say if it is a telling sentence or a question. Tell what end mark should be added.

1. What color is the balloon

2. The balloon has many colors

Write It Now write each sentence correctly.

Example where will the balloon go
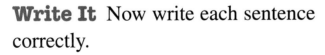
Where will the balloon go?

Write each sentence. Add the correct end mark. Write **T** after each telling sentence and **Q** after each question.

Example A bee is a bug

A bee is a bug. T

1. Do bees buzz

3. Bees have wings

2. Bees make honey

4. Is honey sweet

5–8. Proofread these sentences from a nature guide. Find four mistakes with capital letters and end marks. Write each sentence correctly.

Example is this a spider Is this a spider?

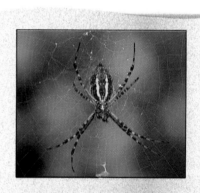

Spiders

a spider has eight legs.

It spins a web

do you know why

Writing Wrap-Up

INFORMING

Write a Nature Guide Page

Write two questions about a bug. Write the answers and draw a picture. Read your questions and answers. Have a classmate check that you used end marks correctly.

8 Commands

One-Minute Warm-Up

Do what this sentence tells you to do.

Close your eyes and count to four.

—from Clap Your Hands, by Lorinda Bryan Cauley

A telling sentence ends with a period. A question ends with a question mark. Another kind of sentence is a **command**. A command tells a person or animal to do something. A command begins with a **capital letter** and ends with a **period**. A command often begins with an action word.

> **P**lay this game with me**.**   **L**isten to the rules**.**

Try It Out

Speak Up Tell how to make each command correct.

1. Hide   **3.** count to ten.

2. be quiet   **4.** Look around

Write It Now write the sentences correctly.

Example close your eyes
Close your eyes.

Write each command correctly.

Example stand here
Stand here.

1. take this rope

2. pull hard

3. do not let go

4–6. Proofread this chart of commands. Find three mistakes with capital letters and end marks. Write the commands correctly.

Example line up at the door? Line up at the door.

Proofreading

Fire Drill Rules

do not talk.

Please walk quickly?

Follow your teacher

WRITING • THINKING • LISTENING • SPEAKING

Writing Wrap-Up

INFORMING

Write Commands

Write commands to use while playing Simon Says. Work with a classmate to check that your commands begin and end correctly. In pairs, read and act out the commands.

9 Exclamations

One-Minute Warm-Up

Say this sentence with surprise or anger in your voice.

"Somebody has been lying in my bed!"

—from Goldilocks and the Three Bears, by James Marshall

All sentences begin with a **capital letter**. A telling sentence and a command end with a period. A question ends with a question mark. Another kind of a sentence is an **exclamation**. It ends with an **exclamation point** (**!**). An exclamation shows a strong feeling such as excitement, surprise, or fear.

Someone broke my chair**!**   **T**here she is**!**

Try It Out

Speak Up Tell how to make each exclamation correct. Read each sentence with strong feeling.

1. help me!
2. I am afraid
3. I must run home now

Write It Now write the exclamations correctly.

Example This bed is too hard This bed is too hard!

Write the correct exclamation in each pair.

Example close the door Close the door!
Close the door!

1. the wolf is after us!
The wolf is after us!

2. I will blow your house down?
I will blow your house down!

3. Go away.
Go away!

4. I am not afraid!
I am not afraid.

5–8. Proofread this page from a class book. Find four mistakes with capital letters and end marks in these exclamations. Write the title and sentences correctly.

Example spider scares little girl.
Spider scares little girl!

Proofreading

Nursery Rhyme News
cow jumps over the moon
big egg falls off the wall!
Mouse runs up the clock?

Writing Wrap-Up

WRITING • THINKING • LISTENING • SPEAKING

CREATING

Write Exclamations

Draw a picture of a nursery rhyme or fairy tale. Write an exclamation about the picture. Read your exclamation with expression to a classmate. Add it to a class book.

For Extra Practice, see page 61.

Enrichment

The Sentence!

Silly Animals

- Fold a sheet of paper. Draw the front part of an animal on the left and the back part of another animal on the right.

- Name your animal and write a sentence about it. Write the naming part on the left and the action part on the right.

Challenge Write a story about your animal. Have a classmate say the naming part and action part of each sentence.

The elephig | plays in mud.

The Sentence Game

Get Ready You will need some paper and 4 blank cards for each player. Write a spelling word on each card. Then write T for telling sentence or Q for question.

T bee

Q dog

How to Play Mix and stack the cards face down. Choose a card and read the word and the letter aloud. Another player writes the word and uses it in a telling sentence or question. Score 1 point for each word spelled correctly. Score 1 point for each complete sentence.

What Is a Sentence? (page 27)

Write sentences by matching the words
in Box A with the words in Box B.

A

1. The plane
2. The ride
3. The food
4. All of us

B

tasted good.

liked the ride.

took off.

was bumpy.

Naming Part and Action Part (pages 29, 31)

Choose a naming part or an action part from the Word
Box to finish each sentence. Write the sentences.

The plane   was setting

5. The sun _____.   6. _____ landed.

Is It a Sentence? (page 33)

Copy each group of words. Write **yes** after each complete
sentence. Write **no** after each group of words that is not
a sentence.

7. Bright lights.   9. I walked home.

8. The city was hot.   10. Made a loud noise.

Which Kind of Sentence? (pages 37, 39, 41)

Write each sentence. Add the correct end mark.
Write **T** after each telling sentence. Write **Q** after
each question.

11. I like the park

12. Will you come

13. Is it fun

14. Children ride bikes

Telling Sentences, Questions, Commands, and Exclamations

(pages 37, 39, 43, 45)

Write each sentence correctly. Add a capital
letter and end mark.

15. can we go to the parade

16. hold my hand

17. that balloon is huge

18. a band plays music

Mixed Review 19–25.

Proofread this report. Find seven mistakes with capital letters and end marks. Be sure to make two word groups into one sentence. Then write the report correctly.

Proofreading Checklist

✔ Do sentences have a naming part and an action part?
✔ Do sentences begin with capital letters?
✔ Do telling sentences and commands end with periods?
✔ Do questions end with question marks?
✔ Do sentences that show strong feeling end with exclamation points?

Example do all birds build nests
Do all birds build nests?

Proofreading

Is It a Bird?

I love birds! Do you like birds. Guess what a bird is. Is a bird an animal that flies?

Not all birds fly. An ostrich and penguin do not fly? An ostrich runs very fast. A penguin. Swims with its short wings.

All birds have feathers. feathers keep a bird warm and dry. No other animals have feathers.

All birds lay eggs. do you want to know more about birds? Look in a bird book

See www.eduplace.com/kids/hme/ for an online quiz.

Test Practice ⭐

Number a sheet of paper from 1 to 6. Read the words next to each number. Decide if the words make a complete sentence that is written correctly. If the words are a correct sentence, write the letter next to "No mistake." If not, write the letter next to the correct answer.

1 cows live on a farm.

  A Cows live on a farm?

  B Cows live on a farm.

  C No mistake

2 Our dog is big

  F Our dog is big.

  G our dog is big.

  H No mistake

3 Ann watched a bird.

  A Ann watched. A bird.

  B ann watched a bird.

  C No mistake

4 The little frog. Hops.

  F The little frog hops?

  G The little frog hops.

  H No mistake

5 A boy walks to school

  A A boy walks to school.

  B A boy walks to school?

  C No mistake

6 Did Jim eat an apple?

  F Did Jim eat an apple.

  G did Jim eat an apple?

  H No mistake

Now write the numbers 7 to 12 on your paper. Read the words next to each number. Decide if the words make a complete sentence that is written correctly. If the words are a correct sentence, write the letter next to "No mistake." If not, write the letter next to the correct answer.

7 The car goes fast.

  A The car goes fast

  B the car goes fast.

  C No mistake

8 Jump over the log

  F jump over the log.

  G Jump over the log.

  H No mistake

9 Bill and Jake. Played ball in the park.

  A Bill and Jake played ball in the park.

  B Bill and Jake played ball in the park?

  C No mistake

10 You did. a great job!

  F You did a great job!

  G you did a great job!

  H No mistake

11 The plants grow tall.

  A The plants grow tall

  B The plants grow tall?

  C No mistake

12 the circus clowns do funny tricks.

  F The circus clowns. Do funny tricks.

  G The circus clowns do funny tricks.

  H No mistake

Extra Practice

(pages 27–28)

1 What Is a Sentence?

Remember

- A sentence tells what someone or something did or does.

●▲ Make sentences by matching sentence parts. Write the sentences.

Example The boy   wagged its tail. The boy drew a dog.
                          drew a dog.

A	**B**
1. Kate	crossed the sky.
2. The rainbow	were red and blue.
3. The colors	painted a picture.

■ Write each sentence, using a sentence part from the Word Box to complete it.

Ryan	swims	kitten
barks	crawls	

Example The puppy _____.
           The puppy barks.

4. _____ has a turtle.

5. His pet turtle _____.

6. My _____ has whiskers.

7. Her fish _____ fast.

(pages 29–30)

2 Naming Part

Remember

- The naming part of a sentence tells who or what did or does something.

●▲ Choose a naming part from the Word Box to begin each sentence. Write the sentences.

Chicks	Bees	Birds	Frogs	Lions

Example _____ peep. Chicks peep.

1. _____ leap.

2. _____ sing.

3. _____ sting.

4. _____ roar.

■ Write each sentence. Draw a line under the naming part.

Example Those snakes hiss. Those snakes hiss.

5. Babies sleep.

6. Children skip.

7. Raindrops drip.

8. Most kittens play.

9. The goat eats hay.

10. Bears growl.

11. Those monkeys howl.

12. Roosters crow.

13. Some farmers hoe.

14. Cows moo and chew.

(pages 31–32)

3 Action Part

- The action part of the sentence tells what the naming part did or does.

Remember

●▲ Write each sentence, using an action part from the Word Box.

naps	shines	hops
chirps	bloom	

Example The rabbit _____.

The rabbit hops.

1. The flowers _____.

2. The sun _____.

3. The robin _____.

4. The cat _____.

■ Write each sentence, adding your own action part.

Example Flowers _____.

Flowers grow in my garden.

5. Bees _____.

6. Birds _____.

7. My friend and I _____.

(pages 33–34)

Remember

4 Is It a Sentence?

- A complete sentence has a naming part and an action part.

●▲ Copy each word group.
Write **yes** if the word group is a sentence.
Write **no** if it is not a sentence.

Example A big park.

   A big park.   no

1. Children played.

2. Two happy boys.

3. Sat on swings.

4. We ran home.

■ Put the naming part and the action part together in the correct order. Write each sentence.

Example loves the rain.
      Brad
      Brad loves the rain.

5. Pam
   wears red boots.

6. fall on us.
   Big raindrops

(pages 37–38)

5 Telling Sentences

- A telling sentence tells something.
- It begins with a capital letter.
- It ends with a period (.).

Remember

●▲ Write the correct telling sentence in each pair.

Example I have a fish. I have a fish.

I have a fish

1. it lives in a fishbowl

   It lives in a fishbowl.

2. The fish has blue stripes

   The fish has blue stripes.

3. It is a zebra fish.

   it is a zebra fish.

4. i like my pet

   I like my pet.

■ Write these telling sentences correctly.

Example joe has a parrot

Joe has a parrot.

5. it has green wings

6. the parrot talks

7. it walks up a ladder

(pages 39–40)

6 Questions

Remember

- A question is a sentence that asks something.
- It begins with a capital letter.
- It ends with a question mark (?).

●▲ Write the correct question in each pair.

Example where is the dog Where is the dog?
    Where is the dog?

1. Is it under the bed?
   is it under the bed?

2. did you call the dog
   Did you call the dog?

3. Did you hear a bark?
   Did you hear a bark

4. is it in the back yard
   Is it in the back yard?

■ Write each question correctly.

Example Do you have a pet
    Do you have a pet?

5. Is it a dog

6. what is its name

7. can it do tricks

(pages 41–42)

7 Which Kind of Sentence?

- A sentence can tell something or ask a question.
- A telling sentence ends with a period.
- A question ends with a question mark.

Remember

●▲ Write each sentence. Add an end mark. Write **T** after each telling sentence. Write **Q** after each question.

Example Do you like kittens

Do you like kittens? Q

1. Lee has a kitten
2. Would you like one
3. Dogs are good pets

4. Do you have a pet
5. What color is your fish
6. It is orange and black

■ Write these as sentences. Use capital letters and end marks correctly.

Example we walk in the woods

We walk in the woods.

7. i like trees in the fall
8. what colors are the leaves

(pages 43–44)

Remember

8 Commands

- A command is a sentence that tells a person or animal to do something.
- It begins with a capital letter and ends with a period.

●▲ Write the correct command in each pair.

Example Listen to the rules. Listen to the rules.
listen to the rules.

1. put the ball here.

   Put the ball here.

2. Dribble the ball.

   Dribble the ball?

3. Run as fast as you can.

   Run as fast as you can

4. aim for the goal

   Aim for the goal.

■ Write the commands correctly.

Example draw some squares.
Draw some squares.

5. toss a stone in a square.

6. hop on one foot

7. Pick up your stone

(pages 45–46)

Remember

⑨ **Exclamations**

- An exclamation is a sentence that shows a strong feeling.
- It begins with a capital letter and ends with an exclamation point (!).

●▲ Write the correct exclamation in each pair. Read the sentence with strong feeling in your voice.

Example I love scary stories I love scary stories!

I love scary stories!

1. this book is great!

   This book is great!

2. I am so afraid?

   I am so afraid!

3. What a neat picture!

   what a neat picture

4. I am so proud of you.

   I am so proud of you!

■ Write each sentence as an exclamation.

Example This story is exciting This story is exciting!

5. the woods are dark

6. the girl is lost

7. A storm is coming

Writing a Personal Narrative

This unit also includes:

Special Focus on Narrating
Writing a Friendly Letter
Page 84

Communication Links
Telling a Story About Yourself
Page 88

Retelling a Spoken Message
Page 90

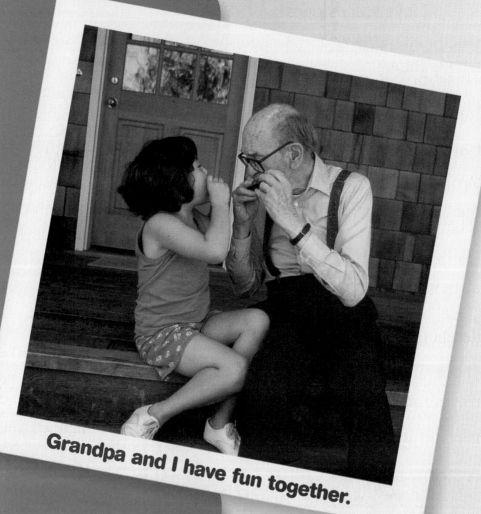

Grandpa and I have fun together.

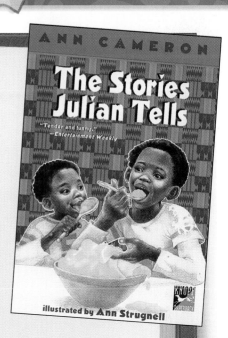

Listening to a Personal Narrative

"Gloria" is a personal narrative about making a new friend. What happened first, next, and last on the day that Julian met Gloria?

Gloria

from The Stories Julian Tells, by Ann Cameron

It happened one afternoon when I was walking down the street by myself. My mother was visiting a friend of hers, and Huey was visiting a friend of his. Huey's friend is five and so I think he is too young to play with. And there aren't any kids just my age. I was walking down the street feeling lonely.

A block from our house I saw a moving van in front of a brown house, and men were carrying in chairs and tables and bookcases and boxes full of I don't know what. I watched for a while, and suddenly I heard a voice right behind me.

See www.eduplace.com/kids/ for information about Ann Cameron.

Unit 2: Personal Narrative

63

"Who are you?"

I turned around and there was a girl in a yellow dress. She looked the same age as me. She had curly hair that was braided into two pigtails with red ribbons at the ends.

"I'm Julian," I said. "Who are you?"

"I'm Gloria," she said. "I come from Newport. Do you know where Newport is?"

I wasn't sure, but I didn't tell Gloria. "It's a town on the ocean," I said.

"Right," Gloria said. "Can you turn a cartwheel?"

She turned sideways herself and did two cartwheels
on the grass.
   I had never tried a cartwheel before, but I tried to
copy Gloria. My hands went down in the grass, my
feet went up in the air, and — I fell over.
   I looked at Gloria to see if she was laughing at me.
If she was laughing at me, I was going to go home
and forget about her.
   But she just looked at me very seriously and said,
"It takes practice," and then I liked her.

Reading As a Writer

Think About the Personal Narrative

- What happened first, next, and last on the day Julian met Gloria?

- What one experience did the story tell about?

- What words did Julian use to name himself in the story?

Think About Writer's Craft

- On page 64, which words give you a picture of what Gloria looks like?

Think About the Picture

- What does the picture on pages 64–65 tell you about what Julian is thinking or feeling as Gloria does a cartwheel?

Responding

Write an answer to this question on another sheet of paper.

- **Personal Response** How did you feel as you read the story? Why?

What Makes a Great Personal Narrative?

A **personal narrative** is a story about you. It tells about something that really happened. When you write a story about yourself, remember to do these things.

▶ Use <u>I</u> and <u>me</u>.

▶ Write about only one thing that happened.

▶ Write enough details to help your reader imagine what happened.

▶ Write about the events in order: first, next, last.

▶ Begin your story in an interesting way. Finish by telling how the story ends or how you felt.

GRAMMAR CHECK

When you write, use complete sentences that begin with a capital letter and end with the correct end mark.

WORKING DRAFT

Read Sarah's personal narrative and what W.R. said about it.

Sarah Rose Manning

> This is a good way to begin.

My New Pet

On Saturday my mom said she would take me to buy a pet. I was so happy! ~~I got up and ate breakfast. First, we went to the drugstore to get shampoo.~~ When we got to the pet shop, I looked at three or four dogs. Then I saw the perfect dog for me.

> What do the dog's fur and your coat look like?

I knew he was the perfect dog for me because his fur was just like my coat. My mom said he was a West Highland white terrier. We bought the dog.

> Why did you name him Peter Rabbit?

We named him Peter Rabbit. That's how I got my pet.

Reading As a Writer

- Which sentences did Sarah take out? Why?
- What changes might Sarah want to make?

Read Sarah's final copy and what W.R. said about it. What did Sarah do to make it better?

> Good, you're using the words <u>I</u> and <u>me</u>.

Peter Rabbit Is a Dog
by Sarah Rose Manning

    On Saturday my mom said she would take me to buy a pet. I was so happy! When we got to the pet shop, I looked at three or four dogs. Then I saw the perfect dog for me. I knew he was the perfect dog for me because his fur was white just like my fake fur coat. I said he was my twin! He also had a big black nose and tiny legs. My mom said he was a West Highland white terrier. We bought the dog.

> This part sounds like you, Sarah.

    When we got home, my dad said that the dog had ears like a rabbit's. We named him Peter Rabbit. When I tell people I have a new pet, I have to explain that Peter Rabbit is a dog!

> This is a good ending.

Reading As a Writer

- What happened first, next, and last in Sarah's story?
- What details did Sarah add about the dog?

See www.eduplace.com/kids/hme/ for more examples of student writing.

Unit 2: Personal Narrative

69

Write a Personal Narrative

▶ Choose Your Topic

1 **List** three things that have happened to you.

2 **Talk** with a classmate about each idea. Answer these questions.

- Which idea does your classmate like best?

- Which idea do you remember best?

Stuck for an Idea?

▶ When were you surprised?
▶ When did you make a friend?
▶ When did you learn something new?

See page 82 for more ideas.

3 **Copy and complete** these sentences. Name your audience and topic.

_____ will read or hear my story.

I will write about _____.

▶ Explore Your Topic

1 **Think** about what your readers will want to know.

2 **Draw** pictures showing what you will write about.

Focus Skill

Telling Enough Details

When you write your story, help your readers imagine what happened by telling enough details. The words <u>what</u>, <u>who</u>, <u>why</u>, <u>when</u>, and <u>where</u> can help you think of details.

Try It Together

Talk with your class about something special that has happened at your school. List details that tell what, who, why, when, and where.

▶ ## Explore Your Story Idea

❶ **Look** back at the pictures you drew for your story. Circle the picture that shows the most important idea.

❷ **Make** a Five W's Chart like this one for your story. Write details to answer the questions.

Five W's Chart
What happened?
Who was there?
Why did it happen?
When did it happen?
Where did it happen?

 See www.eduplace.com/kids/hme/ for graphic organizers.

Unit 2: Personal Narrative

Focus Skill

Keeping to the Topic

Write only about events that are important to the main part of your story. Don't write about things that do not belong in your story.

Try It Together

Write the number of the picture that doesn't show one of the activities at a water park. Talk with your class about how you chose that picture.

1.

water slide

3.

horseback riding

2.

wave pool

4.

inner tubes

▶ Explore Your Story

1 **Use** your Five W's Chart to tell your story to a classmate.

2 **Cross out** details that do not belong.

▶ Plan Your Personal Narrative

① **Look** at how Sarah organized her details.

Five W's Chart
What happened? picked out a dog named him Peter Rabbit went to buy a pet

Sequence Chart
First went to buy a pet
Next picked out a dog
Last named him Peter Rabbit

② **Make** a chart like the one below. Write details from your Five W's Chart in the boxes, showing the order in which the events happened. Include all of your details.

Sequence Chart
First
Next
Last

See www.eduplace.com/kids/hme/
for graphic organizers.

Unit 2: Personal Narrative

▶ Write Your Personal Narrative

Sometimes you write one sentence for each detail. Other times you put more details into one sentence.

Sarah used details from her Sequence Chart to write her story.

Sequence Chart
First
went to buy a pet
my mom and I
Saturday

On Saturday my mom said she would take me to buy a pet.

1 **Use** your Sequence Chart to help you write your story. Use some of the details in your First box to write your beginning sentence.

2 **Use** your other details to help you write the rest of your story. You can write one sentence for each detail or put more details into one sentence.

3 **Use** some of the details in your Last box to write your ending sentence.

How Good Is Your Personal Narrative?

▶ **Read** your draft.

▶ **Copy** the sentences below that describe your personal narrative.

Superstar

☐ My beginning is interesting.

☐ I wrote many details that tell what, who, why, when, and where.

☐ All of my sentences are in order and tell about one main idea.

☐ The last part tells how the story ended, how I felt, or what I learned.

☐ My writing has only a few mistakes.

Rising Star

☐ My beginning could be more interesting.

☐ I need more details that tell what, who, why, when, and where.

☐ Some sentences are out of order or do not tell about my main idea.

☐ The story needs a better ending.

☐ My writing has many mistakes.

See www.eduplace.com/kids/hme/ to interact with this rubric.

Unit 2: Personal Narrative

75

► Revise Your Personal Narrative

1 Look at the sentences from page 75 that you wrote about your personal narrative. What can you do to make your story better?

- Cross out sentences that aren't needed.
- Write another ending. Do you like it better?

2 Have a writing conference.

When You're the Writer

- Write a question about a part of your story that you want help with.

- Read your story to a classmate. Ask your question.

When You're the Listener

- Tell two things you like about the story.

- Ask questions about parts that aren't clear or that could be more interesting.

- Look at the next page for some other ideas.

3 Revise your story.

Think about what you and your classmate talked about. Make changes to your draft. The Revising Strategies on page 78 may help you.

What to Say in a Writing Conference

If you are thinking . . .   **You could say . . .**

Are the events in the right order?

The order of events does not make sense.

Why did you put this part in your story?

This part doesn't belong in the story.

This part is not very clear.

What details could you add to make this part clearer?

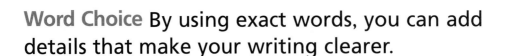

Revising Strategies

Word Choice By using exact words, you can add details that make your writing clearer.

> ran
> Maria and I ~~went~~ inside when it started to rain.
>
> soaked
> My shirt was ~~wet~~.

▶ **Find** one place in your story where you can add details by using an exact word.

📖 Use My First Thesaurus on page H45 to find exact words.

Sentence Fluency Begin sentences in different ways.

> played
> I ~~was~~ an elf in a show at
>
> sneaked
> summer camp. I ~~was supposed to~~
>
> ~~sneak~~ into the shoemaker's shop.

▶ **Draw** a line under the first few words of each sentence in your story. If two or more sentences start the same way, begin them in different ways.

▶ Proofread Your Personal Narrative

❶ Proofread your draft. Use the Proofreading Checklist and the Proofreading Marks.

❷ Use a class dictionary to check spellings.

Proofreading Checklist

☐ Each sentence begins with a capital letter.
☐ Each sentence ends with the correct end mark.
☐ Each sentence has a naming part and an action part.
☐ Each word is spelled correctly.

Proofreading Marks

∧ Add	≡ Capital letter
℘ Delete	/ Small letter
¶ Indent for new paragraph	

Using the Proofreading Marks

Do you know what happened
?
next℘ i called Home.

❸ Review these rules before you proofread.

Grammar and Spelling Connections

Sentences Begin and end sentences correctly.

I was really scared when I moved to our new house. Who would play with me?

Short Vowel Sounds A short vowel sound may be spelled **a**, **e**, **i**, **o**, or **u**.

hat　　　pet　　pin　　　top　　　fun

📖 See the Spelling Guide on page H40.

▶ Publish Your Personal Narrative

1 **Make** a neat final copy of your story.

2 **Write** an interesting title.

3 **Look** at Ideas for Sharing on the next page.

4 **Publish** or share your story in a way that works for your audience.

- Be sure you wrote all letters correctly and used good spacing. Check that you fixed every mistake.
- Begin the first, last, and each important word in your title with a capital letter.

▶ Reflect

Answer these questions about your personal narrative.

- What was easy about writing this story? What was hard?

- What did you learn about writing a story about yourself?

 Do you like this paper better than other papers you have written? Why or why not?

 Tech Tip If you wrote your story on a computer, fix all mistakes. Then print out a final copy.

Ideas for Sharing

Write It

- Send it to someone you know, using e-mail.
- Make it into an accordion book.

Say It

- ★ Read it in the Author's Chair.
- Tell your story as you and some classmates act it out.

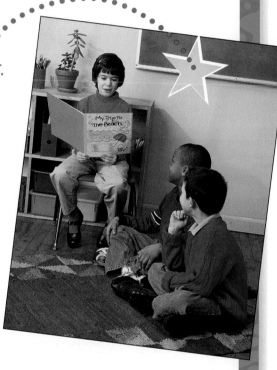

Show It

- Add photos or draw pictures for it.
- Make it into a comic strip.

Speak loudly and clearly when you share your story.

Tech Tip
Use computer clip art to add pictures.

Writing Prompts

Use these prompts for ideas or to practice for a test. Decide who your audience will be and write your narrative in a way that they will understand and enjoy.

1 When did you solve a problem? Write a personal narrative telling about the problem and how you solved it.

2 Write a personal narrative about helping someone. Whom did you help? How? Why? Where and when did you help?

Writing Across the Curriculum

3 **FINE ART**

The people in this painting are riding on a ferry boat. Write a personal narrative about a time you rode on a boat, a bus, a train, or a plane. Who was with you? Where did you go? What did you do?

National Museum of American Art, Washington, D.C./Art Resource

Ferry Boat Trip
William H. Johnson
ca. 1943–1944

See www.eduplace.com/kids/hme/ for more prompts.

Test Practice

Read this writing prompt.

Write a personal narrative about <u>helping</u> <u>someone</u>. Whom did you help? How? Why? Where and when did you help?

Testing

Follow these steps for writing to a prompt.

❶ Look for clues that tell you what to write about. The words <u>helping someone</u> are clues.

❷ Look for questions that you should answer. What questions are in the prompt above?

❸ Plan your writing. Make and fill in a chart like the one at the right.

❹ Look at page 75. What makes a Superstar?

❺ Write your personal narrative.

Answering a Writing Prompt
Clue words: helping someone
My topic:
Whom did you help?
How did you help?
Why did you help?
Where did you help?
When did you help?

Writing a Friendly Letter

You write a **friendly letter** to someone you know. Read Adam's friendly letter and what W.R. said about it.

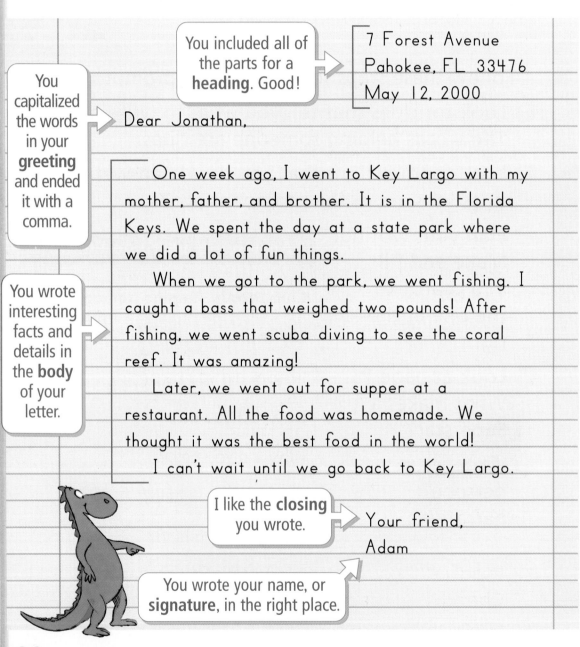

You included all of the parts for a **heading**. Good!

7 Forest Avenue
Pahokee, FL 33476
May 12, 2000

You capitalized the words in your **greeting** and ended it with a comma.

Dear Jonathan,

You wrote interesting facts and details in the **body** of your letter.

One week ago, I went to Key Largo with my mother, father, and brother. It is in the Florida Keys. We spent the day at a state park where we did a lot of fun things.

When we got to the park, we went fishing. I caught a bass that weighed two pounds! After fishing, we went scuba diving to see the coral reef. It was amazing!

Later, we went out for supper at a restaurant. All the food was homemade. We thought it was the best food in the world!

I can't wait until we go back to Key Largo.

I like the **closing** you wrote.

Your friend,
Adam

You wrote your name, or **signature**, in the right place.

- What information is on each line of the **heading**?

- Who will get Adam's letter?

- What did Adam write about in the **body** of his letter?

- What words did Adam use for a **closing**? How did he begin them?

- Where did Adam write his **signature**?

How to Write a Friendly Letter

1 **Choose** a person you want to write to.

2 **List** what you could say in your letter. Circle what you will say and number your ideas in the order you will write about them.

3 **Write** your letter. Include all five parts.

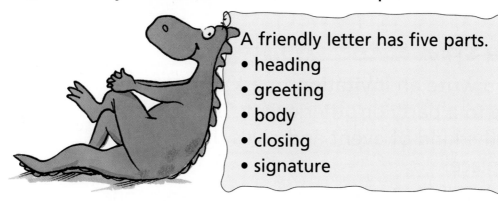

A friendly letter has five parts.
- heading
- greeting
- body
- closing
- signature

4 **Proofread** your letter. Use the Proofreading Checklist on page 79. Use a class dictionary to check your spelling.

⑤ Make a neat final copy of your letter.

⑥ Address the envelope. Remember to add a postage stamp. Look at this envelope that Hannah addressed to her friend.

Your return address is important! →

Hannah White
1 Lenox Way
Pahokee, FL 33476

The mailing address lists everything the letter carrier needs to deliver the letter. →

Anne Marie Igo
29 Argilla Road
Irvine, CA 92606

⑦ Mail your letter.

Remember, you can mail your letter at a post office or in a nearby mailbox.

Other Types of Friendly Letters

You write an **invitation** to ask someone to come to a party or other event. The invitation tells the kind of event and gives the date, time, and place.

Write a **thank-you letter** to thank someone for a gift or for doing something for you.

Read the invitation and the thank-you letter on the next page.

Invitation

63 Dewey Street
Round Rock, TX 78681
October 1, 2000

Dear Auntie Marie,

Please come to my birthday party. I will be seven years old this year.

The party will be at my house on Friday, October 22, at 6:00 in the evening. Please call me to let me know if you can join us.

I hope you can come!

Love,
Bethanie

Thank-you Letter

16 Lime Lane
Boston, MA 02116
August 24, 2000

Dear Max,

Thank you for teaching me how to use my camera last Saturday. I really enjoyed our time together. I have a very funny picture of you at the beach. I will put it in a frame and mail it to you soon.

Sincerely,
Kimi

Telling a Story About Yourself

Lisa told a story about herself. What important things did she do with her voice, face, and hands?

On my birthday, I woke up early. I knew that my mom had a surprise for me!

At breakfast she put an unusual box on the floor. Noises came from the box, so I peeked inside. Can you guess what I saw?

I saw a tiny puppy! He had a small black nose and little floppy ears!

So that's how I got Spike. He's not a puppy now. He is HUGE with a LARGE black nose and BIG floppy ears. Spike is my . . . VERY . . . BEST . . . friend!

Think and Discuss

- How often should a speaker look at the audience?

- What kinds of words and details should a speaker use to make a story clear?

- How can a speaker use his or her voice to make a story interesting?

- How can a speaker use his or her face, hands, and body to keep the audience interested?

Tips for Telling a Story About Yourself

▶ Look at your audience.

▶ Speak clearly and loudly enough for everyone to hear.

▶ Use words that tell exactly what you want to say.

▶ Include details that tell who, what, where, when, why, and how.

▶ Speak with feeling.

▶ Use body language to show how you felt.

Apply It

Plan and tell your classmates a story about something that happened to you. Write your story idea. Make sure you use the tips listed above as you tell your story.

Retelling a Spoken Message

Have you ever listened to a message and then had to retell it to a friend or family member? If so, could you remember the whole message?

When you hear a message, listen carefully for important facts such as names, times, and places.

Try It Together

Discuss with your class what the child says and does.

Tips for Retelling a Spoken Message

▶ Listen to the whole message.

▶ Listen for important facts and details.

▶ Ask questions about facts that are not clear.

▶ Repeat the message right away.

▶ Retell the message to the right person.

Apply It

Work with a small group. First, write a short message. Then tell your message quietly to one person. Listen as he or she asks questions and repeats the message to you. Then listen as he or she retells it to the whole group.

Nouns and Pronouns

Look at these puppets we made!

1 Nouns

Say the words that name people in this sentence.

Our family and friends begin to arrive too.

—from A Birthday Basket for Tía, by Pat Mora

A word that names a person is called a **noun**. Read these sentences. Say the nouns that name people.

My **father** is a **teacher**.

My **mother** is a **dentist**.

Try It Out

Speak Up Tell which words are nouns.

1. The girl claps.

2. A boy cheers.

3. The baby laughs.

Write It Now write the sentences and draw a line under each noun.

Example The mother smiles.

The <u>mother</u> smiles.

Write these sentences. Draw a line under each noun that names a person.

Example The girl has a birthday party.

The girl has a birthday party.

1. The father serves cake.

2. The friends bring gifts.

3–5. Copy the invitation. Draw lines under three nouns that name people.

Example My grandpa chooses songs.

My grandpa chooses songs.

You Are Invited!
Come to music night at my house
this Friday. My mother plays the
piano. My brother plays the drums.
Even the baby sings along!

Writing Wrap-Up

WRITING • THINKING • LISTENING • SPEAKING

INFORMING

Write Sentences

Write sentences about what two or more people in your family like to do. Read the sentences to a classmate. Have the classmate say each noun that names a person.

2 More Nouns

Make up sentences about the picture. Name at least one animal, one place, and one thing.

A noun names a person. A **noun** can also name an animal, a place, or a thing. Read the sentences. Which noun names a place? Which noun names a thing? Which noun names an animal?

Tom went to the **lake**.

A **fish** swam near the **dock**.

Try It Out

Speak Up Read each sentence. Say the noun that names an animal, a place, or a thing.

1. The farm was huge.

2. We saw a horse.

3. Dan drove a truck.

4. I dug up a carrot.

Write It Now write each sentence. Draw a line under the noun that names an animal, a place, or a thing.

Example The barn was red. The <u>barn</u> was red.

Write the sentences. Draw a line under each noun that names a place or a thing.

Example I have a baseball.

I have a <u>baseball</u>.

1. Emma has the bat.

2. We play at school.

3–5. Copy Karen's journal entry. Write a noun from the Word Box to finish each sentence.

Example There is a park near my _____.

There is a park near my school.

| dog |
| school |
| park |
| kite |

I went to the __(3)__ today. I took a __(4)__ to fly. My __(5)__ came along to chase squirrels.

Writing Wrap-Up   WRITING • THINKING • LISTENING • SPEAKING

EXPRESSING

Write a Journal Entry

Write about a place that your family likes. Read your entry aloud. Have a classmate say the nouns and tell whether they name people, animals, places, or things.

For Extra Practice, see page 125.

3 One and More Than One

List things in your classroom. Which words on your list name more than one thing?

A noun can name **more than one** person, animal, place, or thing. Add **s** to most nouns to name more than one. Look at the underlined nouns. Which noun names one? Which noun names more than one?

A <u>swimmer</u> is in the pool.

Two <u>swimmer**s**</u> are racing.

Try It Out

Speak Up Read the sentences. Say the two nouns in each sentence. Tell which one names more than one.

1. The swimmers are at the pool.

2. Two teams will have a race.

3. The racers dive into the water.

4. The winners get a prize.

Write It Now write each sentence. Draw a line under the noun that names more than one.

Example Two flags are by the pool.

Two <u>flags</u> are by the pool.

Write the sentences. Complete each one with the noun that names more than one.

Example The (girl, girls) dive in.

The girls dive in.

1. The (racers, racer) swim fast.

2. The (parent, parents) cheer.

3–6. Proofread this sign. Find four nouns that should name more than one. Write the sign correctly.

Example People must wear cap.

People must wear caps.

Proofreading

Obey All Pool Rule

Swimmer must hang their towel on hooks.

No ball are allowed in the pool.

Do not run near the pool.

Writing Wrap-Up

WRITING • THINKING • LISTENING • SPEAKING

INFORMING

Write School Rules

Write two rules to follow at school. Read your rules to a classmate. Have the classmate tell which nouns name one and which nouns name more than one.

Combining Sentences: Naming Parts

Joining Naming Parts You may write two sentences that have the same action part. Join them to make one longer sentence. Write <u>and</u> between the two **naming parts** and then write the action part.

> **Tasha** went to the pool.
>
> **Deb** went to the pool.
>
> **Tasha** <u>and</u> **Deb** went to the pool.

Try It Out

Speak Up/Write It Read each pair of sentences. Use <u>and</u> to join their naming parts. Then say and write the new longer sentence.

Example The glasses are on the table.
The books are on the table.
The glasses and the books are on the table.

1. Tasha jumped into the pool.
   Deb jumped into the pool.

2. The books got wet.
   The glasses got wet.

Revising Strategies continued

Apply It

1–9. Read Ed's e-mail letter. Copy each pair of underlined sentences. Circle the naming part in each sentence. Then use <u>and</u> to make the two underlined sentences into one. Write each new sentence.

Example <u>My friends saw the boy.</u> <u>I saw the boy.</u>

My friends and I saw the boy.

Revising

Type Face ▼ | Size ▼ | **B** *I* <u>u</u> | Spell Check

Dear Jay,

A little boy ran around the edge of the pool. <u>His mom called to him.</u> <u>His dad called to him.</u> The boy fell into the deep end of the pool.

<u>His dad jumped into the pool.</u> <u>The lifeguard jumped into the pool.</u> Everyone watched. <u>The lifeguard pulled him out.</u> <u>His dad pulled him out.</u>

My parents always say, "Don't run near the pool!" Now I know why!

Ed

4 Nouns with es

One-Minute Warm-Up

Which words name more than one? How do they end?

. . . and boxes and boxes and boxes of hats!

—from Aunt Flossie's Hats (and Crab Cakes Later),
by Elizabeth Fitzgerald Howard

Add <u>s</u> to most nouns to name more than one. Add **es** to nouns that end with <u>s</u>, <u>x</u>, <u>ch</u>, and <u>sh</u> to name **more than one**. Say the nouns that name more than one.

cla<u>ss</u>	fo<u>x</u>	bea<u>ch</u>	wi<u>sh</u>
class**es**	fox**es**	beach**es**	wish**es**

Try It Out

Speak Up Say each sentence, using the noun that names more than one.

1. Maria likes the (dress, dresses).

2. Roberto sees four (watches, watch).

3. Here are some blue (dishes, dish).

Write It Now write the sentences correctly.

Example I see two (box, boxes). I see two boxes.

Write each noun to name more than one.

Example porch porches

1. bench
2. box
3. bush
4. class

5–8. Proofread Suelin's letter. Find four nouns that should end in <u>es</u>. Write the letter correctly.

Example Mom made two lunch.

Mom made two lunches.

Dear Grandma,

Mom and I had a picnic at the beach. We took two buses to get there. We packed four sandwich, three peachs, two glass, and two dishs. We had fun!

Suelin

Writing Wrap-Up   WRITING · THINKING · LISTENING · SPEAKING

NARRATING

Write a Story

Write about a picnic you would like to have with friends. Tell what you would eat and do. Use words such as <u>lunches</u>, <u>peaches</u>, and <u>sandwiches</u>. Read your story to a classmate.

5 Nouns That Change Spelling

Read the sentence. Which nouns name more than one? Which noun does not add <u>s</u> or <u>es</u> to name more than one?

There are many mountains where the children live.

— from <u>Children Around the World</u>, by Lynda Snowdon

Add <u>s</u> or <u>es</u> to most nouns to name more than one. Change the spelling of some nouns to name **more than one**. Look at the pictures and words below. Which nouns name more than one?

child	children

man	men

woman	women

Try It Out

Speak Up Name the group of people in each picture.

1.

2.

3.

Write It Now write these nouns.

Write the sentences correctly.

Example Two (child, children) saw a mule.
Two children saw a mule.

1. Three (man, men) chased the mule.

2. Two (woman, women) caught it.

3–4. Copy this ad. Change the underlined words to name more than one.

Example We need <u>man</u>. We need men.

WANTED: MULE RIDERS

We need <u>child</u> and <u>woman</u>.

YOU MUST LIKE ANIMALS!

Ride A Mule

Writing Wrap-Up

WRITING • THINKING • LISTENING • SPEAKING

PERSUADING

Write an Ad

Write an ad for men, women, or children to help in your class. Tell why it would be fun to help. Read your ad to classmates. Discuss if what you wrote would make someone want to answer the ad.

6 Special Nouns

Name an alphabet letter. Think of a special person, place, and pet name that begin with that letter. Make up a chant like this one.

A, my name is Ann.

I live in Appleton.

My pet's name is Amos.

Some nouns name special people, animals, places, or things. These **special nouns** begin with **capital letters**.

Nouns	Special Nouns
man	**D**ean
street	**E**lm **S**treet
town	**L**akewood
pet	**W**ags

Try It Out

Speak Up Tell which nouns name special people, animals, or places. How do they begin?

1. Deven lives in Farwell.

2. His sister Cora has a cat, Fluffy.

Write It Write the sentences. Begin each special noun correctly.

Example I live in vermont. I live in Vermont.

3. My friend marta writes to me.

4. She moved to texas last year.

Write the sentences. Begin each special noun correctly.

Example Where is eric today?

Where is Eric today?

1. He went to dallas.

2. He took his dog, chip.

3–6. Proofread this poster. Find four mistakes with capital letters. Write the poster correctly.

Example We looked all over portland.

We looked all over Portland.

Proofreading

LOST CAT

Have you seen harry, our cat?

His home is on east street.

Please call greg or Cindy

at 555-6135.

Writing Wrap-Up   WRITING · THINKING · LISTENING · SPEAKING

INFORMING

Write Sentences for a Poster

Make a poster for a lost animal. Write the animal's name and where it lives. Draw a picture. Show and read your poster. Have classmates name the special nouns.

7 Pronouns

Play the game I Spy. Think of clues like the ones on the poster. Use <u>he</u>, <u>she</u>, <u>it</u>, and <u>they</u> in your clues.

> I spy somebody.
> She has brown hair.
> She is wearing jeans.
> Who is she?

A **noun** names a person, an animal, a place, or a thing. A **pronoun** can take the place of a noun.

The **plane** lands.	**Jill** looks.	**Jeff** stands.	**Jeff** and **Jill** go.
It lands.	**She** looks.	**He** stands.	**They** go.

Try It Out

Speak Up Name the pronoun in the Word Box that can take the place of the underlined noun or nouns in each sentence.

It	She
They	He

1. <u>Steve</u> and <u>Betsy</u> made bread.

2. <u>Betsy</u> warmed milk.

3. <u>Steve</u> added flour.

4. The <u>bread</u> baked in the oven.

Write It Now write each sentence, using a pronoun from the Word Box in place of the underlined noun or nouns.

Example <u>Betsy</u> likes bread. She likes bread.

Write each sentence. Use a pronoun from the
Word Box to take the place of the underlined noun.

> They
>
> She
>
> He

Example <u>Toys</u> are on the rug.

>   They are on the rug.

1. <u>Tony</u> picks up toys.

2. <u>Lucy</u> cleans the rug.

3–4. Proofread Emily's note. Find two mistakes in using
pronouns. Copy the note correctly.

Example Matt swept the floor. It used a broom.

>   Matt swept the floor. He used a broom.

Mom,

Tim put the dishes away. They was
careful. The kitchen is clean now.
He looks spotless.

>   Emily

Writing Wrap-Up   WRITING • THINKING • LISTENING • SPEAKING

INFORMING

Write a Message

Write a phone message. Tell who called, for whom, and what
he or she wanted. Use <u>he</u>, <u>she</u>, <u>it</u>, or <u>they</u>. Read the message
aloud. Have a classmate name the pronouns.

Writing Clearly with Nouns and Pronouns

Using Pronouns When you write, try not to use the same **naming part** over and over again. Use a **pronoun** to take its place. This will make your writing better.

> **Gina and Ben** do jobs. **Gina and Ben** help.

> **Gina and Ben** do jobs. **They** help.

Try It Out

Speak Up Read the poster. Find the naming part that is repeated in each numbered pair of sentences. Use a pronoun in place of the naming part in the second sentence. Say the new sentence.

Is your car dirty?

(1.) Gina and Ben will wash it.
   Gina and Ben will wax it too!

(2.) Your car will sparkle.
   Your car will look like new.

Write It 1–2. Now write the two new sentences you said.

Example Ben drew the poster.
   Ben painted it.
   He painted it.

Revising Strategies continued

Apply It

1–2. Read this part of an ad. Find the sentence with a naming part that is repeated. Copy that sentence and circle the naming part. Then use a pronoun in place of the naming part. Write the new sentence.

Example Mr. Smith saw the ad.
Mr. Smith called right away.

(Mr. Smith) called right away. He called right away.

Revising

Doggy Daycare

Mary and Dan will care for your dog.
Mary and Dan will walk your pup.

3–4. Now read the rest of the ad. Find the sentence with a naming part that is repeated. Copy that sentence and circle the naming part. Then use a pronoun in place of the naming part. Write the new sentence.

Revising

Mary will teach your dog to roll over.
Mary will teach your dog tricks.
Call Mary or Dan at 625-1478.

8 Naming Yourself Last

Say the naming part of the sentence. What person is named last? Say another sentence, using <u>Abuela and I</u>.

Abuela and I are always going places.

—from <u>Abuela</u>, by Arthur Dorros

When you write or talk about another person and yourself, **name yourself last**. Always use the word <u>I</u> in the naming part of the sentence.

Tina and **I** rode our new bikes.

Try It Out

Speak Up Tell how to make the sentences correct.

1. I and Carl ran a race.

2. Me and Amy jumped rope.

3. I and Chen flew a kite.

Write It Now write the sentences correctly.

Example Ann and me played.

Ann and I played.

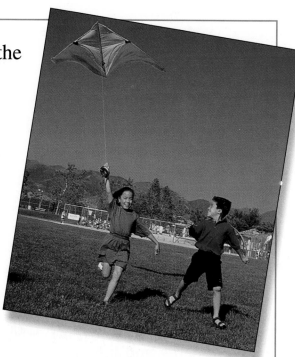

Write the sentences correctly.

Example I and Jane paint. Jane and I paint.

1. Taro and me sing.

2. I and Liz run.

3–6. Proofread this poem. Find four mistakes in using pronouns. Write the poem correctly.

Example Me and Carlos play ball.

Carlos and I play ball.

Proofreading

My Friends

I and Tía like to swim.

Me and Lynn like to walk.

I and Rico play soccer.

But Stan and me just talk.

Writing Wrap-Up

WRITING • THINKING • LISTENING • SPEAKING

CREATING

Write a Poem

Write a poem about what you do with friends. Use each friend's name and then <u>I</u>. Listen as classmates read their poems. Did they name themselves last?

9 Nouns Ending with 's

One-Minute Warm-Up

Read the sentence. Whose parents are named? Julius is a pig that Maya owns. What two words could you say to show this?

Maya's parents didn't think that they would like Julius.

—from Julius by Angela Johnson

Some nouns show that a person or animal owns or has something. When a noun names one person or animal, add an **apostrophe** (') and **s** to that noun to **show ownership**.

girl**'s** pet   Sam**'s** hamster   owl**'s** wing

Try It Out

Speak Up Tell what to add to each noun in ( ) to make it correctly show ownership. Read each pair of nouns.

1. (bird) cage
2. (Sara) puppy
3. (owl) beak
4. (dog) nose

Write It Now write each pair of nouns correctly.

Example (dog) leash dog's leash

Write the sentence in each pair with a
noun that correctly shows ownership.

Example Sue mice are cute. Sue's mice are cute.

            Sue's mice are cute.

1. A boy's bird got loose.
  A boy bird got loose.

2. Toms dog did tricks.
  Tom's dog did tricks.

3–6. Proofread these judge's notes. Find four nouns with
mistakes in showing ownership. Write the notes correctly.

Example Pablo fish won second prize.

            Pablo's fish won second prize.

Proofreading

The best trick was done by Megs puppy.

Ben kitten has the softest fur.

The prize for the biggest pet should go to Marco dog.

Kims snake is the longest pet.

Writing Wrap-Up WRITING • THINKING • LISTENING • SPEAKING

COMPARING &
CONTRASTING

Write a Paragraph

Write about two children and the pets they own. Tell how the
pets are alike and different. Read your paragraph. Have a
classmate tell which nouns show ownership.

10 Nouns Ending with s'

Read the words. To whom do the kites belong? Who owns the books? To whom do the nests belong? Use the words in sentences.

boys' kites

girls' books

birds' nests

A noun that names one person or animal ends with an apostrophe and s to show ownership. When a noun names more than one and ends in s, add just an **apostrophe** (') after the s to **show ownership**. The underlined nouns name more than one. What was added to show ownership? Where was it added?

two <u>boys'</u> closets   <u>birds'</u> nests   <u>twins'</u> room

Try It Out

Speak Up Each underlined noun names more than one. Tell what you must add to make these nouns show ownership. Read the word groups.

1. four <u>boys</u> caps   3. <u>friends</u> books
2. <u>kittens</u> box   4. <u>cousins</u> dogs

Write It Now write each group of words above. Make the underlined noun show ownership.

Example two <u>girls</u> dresses   two girls' dresses

The underlined nouns name more than one. Write the sentences, adding an apostrophe to each underlined noun to show ownership.

Example My <u>aunts</u> barn is full. My aunts' barn is full.

1. The <u>hens</u> cages are in one corner.

2. My <u>brothers</u> bikes are here too.

3–5. Proofread Tanya's list. Find three mistakes with nouns that name more than one and that show ownership. Write the list correctly.

Example I will pick up my brothers books.

I will pick up my brothers' books.

Proofreading

I will wash the cats dishes.

I will make my sisters beds.

I will put away the twins toys.

Writing Wrap-Up   WRITING • THINKING • LISTENING • SPEAKING

NARRATING

Write a Story

Write about girls' pets, friends' kites, or boys' hats. Read your story. Have a classmate draw a picture of it. Name the nouns that show ownership in each of your stories.

Exact Nouns

Nouns name people, animals, places, and things. When you write, choose nouns that give lots of information. Use **exact nouns** to paint a picture in your reader's mind and to make your writing more interesting.

The <u>animal</u> sleeps.
The **kitten** sleeps.

I eat <u>fruit</u>.
I eat an **apple**.

Apply It

Writing Exact Nouns 1–3. Read and copy this poster. Write an exact noun from the box in place of each underlined noun. Use your dictionary for help.

Example You will see a <u>horse</u>.
You will see a pony.

| goldfish |
| pony |
| puppy |
| parrot |

Pet Show Today

You will see a <u>bird</u>,
a <u>dog</u>, and a <u>fish</u>.
Please join our class!

Enrichment

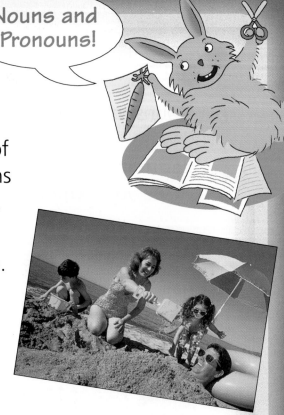

Picture Names

- Cut out a picture from a magazine. Paste it on a sheet of paper. On the back, write nouns for the people, animals, places, and things in the picture.

- Trade pictures with a classmate. Make a list of nouns in your classmate's picture. Look at your classmate's list. Did you both write the same nouns?

Buddy Books

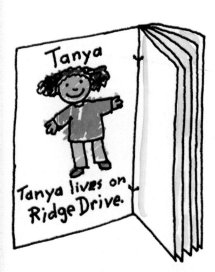

Tanya

Tanya lives on Ridge Drive.

Make a book with three sheets of paper. Write a friend's name on each page. Draw a picture of the friend. Then write a sentence under the picture that tells where your friend lives.

Challenge Use the telephone book to find your friends' telephone numbers. Add them to your buddy book.

Nouns (pages 93, 95)

Write the sentences. Draw a line under each noun. Tell if the noun names a person, an animal, a place, or a thing.

1. We swam in the lake.

2. We slept in a tent.

3. My father cooked.

4. Our dog went with us.

One and More Than One (page 97)

Write each sentence, using the noun that names more than one.

5. Three (boats, boat) went by.

6. I ate two (apple, apples).

7. We read some (book, books).

Nouns with es (page 101)

Write each noun to name more than one.

8. dish   10. fox

9. bus   11. lunch

Nouns That Change Spelling (page 103)

Write each noun to name more than one.

12. child   13. man

Special Nouns (page 105)
Write the sentences, using a capital letter for each special noun.

14. My brother is called rusty.

15. Our house is on oak road.

Pronouns (page 107)
Write each sentence. Use one of the pronouns in ( ) to take the place of the underlined words.

16. <u>Jenny and Paul</u> hiked up the hill. (It, She, They)

17. <u>The hill</u> was very high.   (He, It, They)

Naming Yourself Last (page 111)
Write the sentences correctly.

18. (Lee and I, I and Lee) ran in a race.

19. (Ed and me, Ed and I) read books.

Nouns Ending with 's and s' (pages 113, 115)
Write each word group. Make the first noun show ownership.

20. mom pan

21. two boys kites

Mixed Review

22–28. Proofread this sports article. Find five mistakes with nouns, one mistake with pronouns, and one mistake with naming yourself last. Write the article correctly.

Proofreading Checklist

✔ Do the names of special people and places begin with capital letters?

✔ Do nouns that name more than one end with <u>s</u> or <u>es</u>?

✔ Are the correct pronouns used to take the place of nouns?

✔ Is an apostrophe and <u>s</u> added to a noun that names one to show ownership?

✔ When naming another person and yourself, is the word <u>I</u> used last?

Example Davids goal won the game.

David's goal won the game.

Proofreading

Our soccer team's first game was last week. We played a team from oakville. It was a close game. Our team won! David scored the winning goal. It was very happy. Me and Carmen also scored goals. All the children played hard.

Our team has two new coach and a new goalie named sandra. Our teams next game is on Saturday at the field on Main street. Come and watch us play.

Test Practice ✦

Number a sheet of paper from 1 to 6. Read each sentence. Decide which type of mistake, if any, appears in the sentence. Write the letter next to the correct answer.

1 I will feed Sams puppy.

  A Spelling

  B Capitalization

  C Punctuation

  D No mistake

2 Bob and mary walk home.

  F Spelling

  G Capitalization

  H Punctuation

  J No mistake

3 She held two boxs.

  A Spelling

  B Capitalization

  C Punctuation

  D No mistake

4 He lives on Elm street.

  F Spelling

  G Capitalization

  H Punctuation

  J No mistake

5 Jan watched the plane.

  A Spelling

  B Capitalization

  C Punctuation

  D No mistake

6 I like my new school?

  F Spelling

  G Capitalization

  H Punctuation

  J No mistake

Now write the numbers 7 to 12 on your paper. Read each sentence. Decide which type of mistake, if any, appears in the sentence. Write the letter next to the correct answer.

7 The cats hide in the bushs.

   A Spelling

   B Capitalization

   C Punctuation

   D No mistake

8 We had a picnic at the beach in July?

   F Spelling

   G Capitalization

   H Punctuation

   J No mistake

9 Where is the man's hat?

   A Spelling

   B Capitalization

   C Punctuation

   D No mistake

10 We moved to texas.

   F Spelling

   G Capitalization

   H Punctuation

   J No mistake

11 I like to read bookes about pets.

   A Spelling

   B Capitalization

   C Punctuation

   D No mistake

12 My dog is named max.

   F Spelling

   G Capitalization

   H Punctuation

   J No mistake

(pages 93–94)

Remember

1 Nouns

- A word that names a person is called a noun.

●▲ Write the sentences. Draw a line under each noun that names a person.

Example A dancer leaped.

A <u>dancer</u> leaped.

1. The teacher watched.

2. A man played music.

3. The baby clapped.

■ **4–13.** Copy the box. Around the box, write each noun that names a person.

Example doctor

Nouns for People

help

doctor

uncle   nurse

mother   girl

under   dentist

Nouns for People

friend   father

looking   where

boy   playmate

drive   baker

(pages 95–96)

Remember

2 More Nouns

- A noun can name a person, an animal, a place, or a thing.

●▲ Write the sentences. Draw a line under each noun that names an animal, a place, or a thing.

Example We went to a farm.
We went to a <u>farm</u>.

1. We saw farmers and cows.

2. We walked by a huge field.

3. The corn grew tall.

■ Write the noun in each row.

Example take   glass   sit   glass

4.	go	like	pig
5.	town	eat	small
6.	send	football	over
7.	bed	keep	hear
8.	see	street	live
9.	three	ate	mom
10.	egg	brown	was

(pages 97–98)

3 One and More Than One

- A noun can name more than one person, animal, place, or thing.
- Add <u>s</u> to most nouns to name more than one.

Remember

●▲ Write the sentences correctly. Use nouns that name more than one.

Example We have two (garden, gardens)

We have two gardens.

1. Many (plants, plant) grow there.

2. One garden has (bean, beans).

3. The other one has (flowers, flower).

4. Chris and Rob grow (tulip, tulips).

5. Lisa grows (carrots, carrot).

6. Does your garden have (weed, weeds)?

■ Write each noun to name more than one.

Example car cars

7. desk
8. clock
9. lamp
10. chair

11. cat
12. pond
13. boy
14. girl

(pages 101–102)

Remember

4 **Nouns with es**

• Add <u>es</u> to nouns that end in <u>x</u>, <u>ch</u>, <u>sh</u>, or <u>s</u> to name more than one.

●▲ Write each sentence, using the noun that names more than one.

Example The (box, boxes) were stacked.
The boxes were stacked.

1. The workers ate their (lunch, lunches).

2. They painted two (benches, bench).

3. They painted three (porches, porch).

4. Then they cleaned all the (brush, brushes).

■ Write each noun to name more than one.

Example one bus   two _____ buses

5. one fox   two _____

6. one dish   five _____

7. one patch   three _____

8. one glass   four _____

9. one inch   ten _____

(pages 103–104)

Remember

5 Nouns That Change Spelling

- Some nouns change their spelling to name more than one.

●▲ Write each sentence, using the correct noun.

Example All of the (child, children) watched the game.

All of the children watched the game.

1. Today two (man, men) played tennis.

2. One (man, men) kept score.

3. Four (woman, women) played later.

4. Some (child, children) will play tomorrow.

■ Write each sentence, using the correct noun from the Word Box.

Example

| man |
| men |

Two of my teachers are _____.

Two of my teachers are men.

| man |
| men |

5. My art teacher is a _____.

| child |
| children |

6. Many _____ like art class.

| woman |
| women |

7. Men and _____ are artists.

Remember

(pages 105–106)

6 Special Nouns

- Begin the names of special people, animals, places, and things with capital letters.

●▲ Write each sentence, using a capital letter to begin each special noun.

Example We moved to elm lane.

We moved to Elm Lane.

1. We live in wilton.

2. My new friend is ben.

3. His pony is named blaze.

■ Write the sentences correctly.

Example My pen pal is john.

My pen pal is John.

4. He lives in dallas.

5. His house is on park road.

6. His fish is named goldie.

(pages 107–108)

7 Pronouns

Remember

- A pronoun can take the place of a noun.
- <u>They</u>, <u>he</u>, <u>she</u> and <u>it</u> are pronouns.

●▲ Chose the correct pronoun to take the place of the underlined word or words. Write each sentence.

Example <u>Stan</u> drove his car.

He They It

He drove his car.

1. <u>Mary</u> went with him.

She   He   It

2. <u>The car</u> had a flat tire.

He   She   It

3. <u>Stan and Mary</u> fixed it.

It   They   He

■ Write each sentence, using a pronoun from the Word Box to take the place of the underlined word or words.

He	She	It	They

Example <u>Raul and Maria</u> visited me.

They visited me.

4. <u>Maria</u> enjoyed the visit.

5. <u>Raul</u> wrote a thank-you note.

(pages 111–112)

8 Naming Yourself Last

- When you write or talk about another person and yourself, name yourself last.
- Use the word <u>I</u> in the naming part of the sentence.

●▲ Choose the words in ( ) that are correct. Then write each sentence.

Example (I and Alice, Alice and I) fish.
  Alice and I fish.

1. (Kate and I, I and Kate) skate.

2. (Me and Nora, Nora and I) play ball.

3. (Pablo and I, Pablo and me) collect stamps.

4 (I and Randy, Randy and I) go swimming.

5. (Carmen and I, I and Carmen) ride bikes.

■ **6–8.** Find three sentences that are not correct. Write them correctly.

Example I and Doug go shopping.
  Doug and I go shopping.

I and my sister like horses.

Sarah and I play the piano.

Ben and me are friends.

Me and Paulo have pet birds.

(pages 113–114)

⑨ Nouns Ending with 's

- When a noun names one person or animal, add an apostrophe (') and <u>s</u> to that noun to show ownership.

● ▲ Change each underlined noun to show ownership. Then write each group of words correctly.

Example <u>Jack</u> sister Jack's sister

1. <u>horse</u> saddle

3. <u>boy</u> food

2. <u>girl</u> boots

4. <u>Carla</u> brush

■ Change the noun in ( ) to show ownership. Write each sentence correctly.

Example A (cat) paw is hurt. A cat's paw is hurt.

5. (Emma) uncle is a vet.

6. Her (uncle) office is busy.

7. A (boy) dog had puppies.

(pages 115–116)

10 Nouns Ending with s'

- When a noun ends in <u>s</u> and names more than one person or animal, add just an apostrophe (') to that noun to show ownership.

Remember

●▲ Write the group of words that has a noun that names more than one and that shows ownership.

Example fathers books fathers' books

fathers' books

1. cousins' football

   cousins football

2. monkey tails

   monkeys' tails

3. friends' party

   friends party

4. foxes dens

   foxes' dens

■ Each noun in ( ) names more than one. Change this noun to show ownership. Write each sentence correctly.

Example I found the (twins) ball. I found the twins' ball.

5. Have you seen my (parents) keys?

6. We searched my (sisters) room.

7. Did they fall in the (dogs) bowl?

Writing a Story

This unit also includes:

Surprise! The hay is a bride and groom.

Listening to a Story

The Wolf's Chicken Stew is a story about a character with a problem. Who is the character? What is the problem?

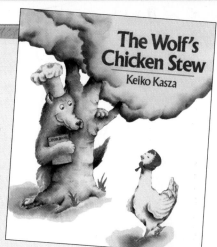

The Wolf's Chicken Stew

by Keiko Kasza

There once lived a wolf who loved to eat more than anything else in the world. As soon as he finished one meal, he began to think of the next.

One day the wolf got a terrible craving for chicken stew.

All day long he walked across the forest in search of a delicious chicken. Finally he spotted one.

"Ah, she is just perfect for my stew," he thought.

The wolf crept closer. But just as he was about to grab his prey . . . he had another idea.

"If there were just some way to fatten this bird a little more," he thought, "there would be all the more stew for me."

So . . . the wolf ran home to his kitchen and he began to cook.

See www.eduplace.com/kids/ for information about Keiko Kasza.

Unit 4: Story   **135**

First he made a hundred scrumptious pancakes. Then, late at night, he left them on the chicken's porch.

"Eat well, my pretty chicken," he cried. "Get nice and fat for my stew!"

The next night he brought a hundred scrumptious doughnuts.

"Eat well, my pretty chicken," he cried. "Get nice and fat for my stew!"

And on the next night he brought a scrumptious cake weighing a hundred pounds.

"Eat well, my pretty chicken," he cried. "Get nice and fat for my stew!"

At last, all was ready. This was the night he had been waiting for. He put a large stew pot on the fire and set out joyfully to find his dinner.

"That chicken must be as fat as a balloon by now," he thought. "Let's see."

But as he peeked into the chicken's house . . . the door opened suddenly and the chicken screeched, "Oh, so it was you, Mr. Wolf!"

"Children, children! Look, the pancakes and the doughnuts and that scrumptious cake . . . All those presents were from Uncle Wolf!"

The baby chicks jumped all over the wolf and gave him a hundred kisses.

"Oh, thank you, Uncle Wolf! You're the best cook in the world!"

Uncle Wolf didn't have chicken stew that night but Mrs. Chicken fixed him a nice dinner anyway.

"Aw, shucks," he thought, as he walked home, "maybe tomorrow I'll bake the little critters a hundred scrumptious cookies!"

Reading As a Writer

Think About the Story

- Which character had a problem? What was the problem?

- How did Mrs. Chicken help the character solve the problem?

- What happened at the beginning, in the middle, and at the end of the story?

Think About Writer's Craft

- How does the writer show you the exact words the characters say?

- What does Mr. Wolf say three times? Why?

Think About the Picture

- How does the picture on page 137 help you know how Mr. Wolf is feeling as Mrs. Chicken opens the door?

Responding

Write an answer to this question.

- **Personal Response** What part of the story did you find most interesting or exciting? Why?

What Makes a Great Story?

A **story** is a tale with a beginning, a middle, and an end. Stories are make-believe, but they may seem real. When you write a story, remember to do these things.

▶ Write an interesting beginning sentence.

▶ Make sure that your story has a beginning, middle, and end, and that the events are in order.

▶ Include interesting details about the setting, characters, and their problem.

▶ Finish your story by telling how the problem is solved and how the story ends.

GRAMMAR CHECK

Use the correct pronoun when replacing a noun in your story.

Kelly O'Masta

WORKING DRAFT

Read Kelly's make-believe story and what W.R. said about it.

> This is a good beginning!

Super Soccer Star

It had been a long, tough season for the Cavalier soccer team. The coach kept reminding the kids to watch the ball and the other team members at all times. He wanted the players to spread out and pass the ball. The players didn't listen to him. They weren't even paying attention to the game. ~~Instead, many of them played with the team mascot.~~

> Can you tell more about the characters?

Kelly and Elizabeth were good players. Keegan was a good player too, but he did not like being the goalie.

Before the last game, the coach got the Cavaliers in a huddle on the soccer field. He told them to play like a team and they would do fine. The team they were playing was big and fast. They quickly scored a goal.

Now the Cavaliers really wanted to win. The team charged down the field. ~~Michael, Anthony, and Jonathan~~ The forwards tried to score lots of times, and Keegan stopped two shots at his goal. Finally, Elizabeth was able to make a goal. The score was tied.

When the second half began, everyone was scrambling for the ball. Kelly remembered not to bunch up. She ran ahead and got open for a pass. Elizabeth made a perfect pass right to her. Kelly scored the winning goal, and the Cavaliers won the game.

What made the Cavaliers start playing better?

The events in your story are in an order that makes sense.

Reading As a Writer

- Why do you think W.R. wanted to know more about the characters?
- What other details could Kelly write about her characters?
- Where does Kelly's story take place?

FINAL COPY

Read Kelly's final copy and what W.R. said.

Playing Like a Team
by Kelly O'Masta

It had been a long, tough season for the Cavalier soccer team. They had played nine games but hadn't won any. The coach kept reminding the kids to watch the ball and the other team members at all times. His favorite words were, "Don't bunch up!" He wanted the players to spread out and pass the ball. They didn't listen to him. They weren't even paying attention to the game.

> Knowing more about the characters helps me understand the story better.

Kelly and Elizabeth were good players, but they spent too much time talking. They laughed loudly, did cartwheels, danced, and chased each other around. Keegan was a good player too, but he did not like being the goalie. He was tall enough, but he often played with the net and did chin-ups on the bar.

Before the last game, the coach got the Cavaliers in a huddle on the soccer field. He told them to play like a team and they would do fine. The team they were playing was big and fast. They quickly scored a goal. It seemed that things couldn't get worse, but they did.

Just before halftime, the coach tripped and fell. Everyone thought he had broken his ankle. An ambulance came. Before the coach was put in the ambulance, he asked the team to gather around him. He said, "Play like a team and you will be fine."

Now the Cavaliers really wanted to win. The team charged down the field. They tried to remember to spread out and pass the ball. The forwards tried to score lots of times, and Keegan stopped two shots at his goal. Finally, Elizabeth was able to make a goal. The score was tied.

When the second half began, everyone was scrambling for the ball. Kelly remembered not to bunch up. She ran ahead and got open for a pass. Elizabeth made a perfect pass right to her. Kelly scored the winning goal, and the Cavaliers won the game. Playing like a team really paid off!

> You added interesting information here telling why the team began to play better.

> I like the sentence you added to end your story.

Reading As a Writer

- What did W.R. like about Kelly's final copy?
- What was the team's problem? How did they solve it?
- Why is the last sentence a good ending?

 See www.eduplace.com/kids/hme/ for more examples of student writing.

Unit 4: Story   **143**

Write a Story

▶ Choose Your Main Character

❶ List three make-believe characters that you could write about in a story.

❷ Think about the characters you listed.

- Which character could you write the most interesting story about?

- Which one would your audience like to read about?

❸ Copy and complete this sentence.

My main character will be a _____ named _____.

HELP ? **Stuck for an Idea?**

How about these characters?

▶ a wild animal
▶ an insect
▶ a snowman
▶ a princess

▶ Choose Your Setting

❶ List two places where your story could take place.

❷ Talk with a classmate about your main character and the settings you have listed. Decide which setting will work better for your character.

❸ Copy and complete this sentence.

My story will take place in a _____ called _____.

Focus Skill

Choosing a Problem

A good story has an interesting problem for the main character to solve. The way a character solves a problem helps to make the story interesting for the reader.

Try It Together

Plan a story about a child at recess. Talk with your class about different problems that the child might have to solve. How could each problem be solved?

▶ Choose Your Story Idea

❶ Think about your main character and setting.

❷ Make a chart like the one below. List two problems you could write about in your story. Then list a way that each problem could be solved.

Possible Problem	Possible Solution

❸ Mark the problem you will write about.

Focus Skill

Developing Characters

Write about your characters so that your readers get to know them.

Look at this character web that Kelly made. It organizes details about one of her characters.

Sometimes you can show what characters are like with the words they say.

looks?

tall

character:
Keegan

does?

plays with the soccer net

does chin-ups on the bar

feels?

doesn't feel like being the goalie

Try It Together

With your class, make character webs about favorite characters from books.

▶ Explore Your Characters

❶ **List** the characters that you will put in your story.

❷ **Make** character webs. Write details telling what your characters look like, what they do, and how they feel.

See www.eduplace.com/kids/hme/ for graphic organizers.

Focus Skill

Mapping Your Story

Use a story map to plan what will happen at the beginning, middle, and end of your story.

Try It Together

With your class, make a story map of The Wolf's Chicken Stew.

▶ **Plan Your Story**

1 **Make** a story map like the one below.

2 **Write** your story events in order.

Introduce your characters, setting, and the problem at the beginning.

The characters work at solving the problem in the middle.

The story ends with the problem being solved.

Story Map
Beginning
Middle
End

 See www.eduplace.com/kids/hme/ for graphic organizers.

Unit 4: Story   **147** ⇨

Focus Skill

Beginning Your Story

Beginning your story with something surprising or puzzling will make your readers want to keep reading.

Weak Beginning	Strong Beginning
Mariel and Luís lost their cat.	Yesterday, Mariel and Luís knew something was wrong.

Try It Together

Work with your class to write a strong beginning for the story of The Three Little Pigs, or another story you know.

▶ ## Write Your Story

❶ **Look** at the first box on your story map. Write two strong beginnings.

❷ **Mark** the one you like better.

❸ **Copy** the beginning you marked onto another sheet of paper.

❹ **Use** your story map and character webs to draft the rest of your story.

Remember: You may want to write the words your characters say.

How Good Is Your Story? ✦

▶ **Copy** the sentences below that tell about your draft.

Superstar

- ☐ My beginning sentence is interesting. It makes my reader want to read more.
- ☐ My story has a beginning, middle, and end. The events are in order.
- ☐ My story has interesting details about the setting, characters, and their problem.
- ☐ The ending tells how the problem is solved and how the story ends.
- ☐ My story has only a few mistakes.

Rising Star

- ☐ My beginning sentence could be better.
- ☐ Story events are missing or out of order.
- ☐ I could add more details about the setting, characters, or problem.
- ☐ My ending needs to tell how the problem is solved and what happens as the story ends.
- ☐ My story has many mistakes.

See www.eduplace.com/kids/hme/ to interact with this rubric.

Unit 4: Story   **149**

▶ Revise Your Story

1 Look at the sentences from page 149 that you wrote about your story. What do you need to do to make your story better?

2 Have a writing conference.

When You're the Writer

- Write a question about a part of your story that you need help with.

- Share your story and your question with a classmate.

When You're the Listener

- Tell two things you like about the story.

- Ask about parts that are not clear.

- Look at the next page for other ideas.

3 Revise your story. Think about what you and your classmate talked about. Make changes to your draft. The Revising Strategies on page 152 may help you.

- Write a new beginning or ending.
- Change the order of events so that they make more sense.
- Add details to help your readers know the characters better.

What to Say in a Writing Conference

If you are thinking . . .

These characters are not very interesting.

I'm not sure what the setting is like.

The ending doesn't tell how the problem was solved.

You could say . . .

What interesting details can you add about the characters?

What other exact words could you use to describe the setting?

What can you add to the ending to explain how the problem was solved?

Revising Strategies

Word Choice Use adverbs in your sentences to help your readers know **how** an action was done.

> slowly
> Jay walked ∧ past the toy store window. He
>   loudly
> watched the toy bear bang ∧ on its drum.

▶ Draw lines under action verbs in your story.
   Add adverbs to tell how the actions were done.

📖 Use the Grammar Glossary on page H35 to learn more about adverbs.

Sentence Fluency Break long, stringy sentences into shorter ones.

> Andy and Meg went to the beach
>   They
> and sat on the sand. ~~and~~ watched
>   ∧
> the gulls and the waves.

▶ Find and fix stringy sentences in your story.

▶ Proofread Your Story

1 **Proofread** your story. Use the Proofreading Checklist and the Proofreading Marks.

2 **Use** a class dictionary to check spellings.

Proofreading Checklist

- Each sentence begins with a capital letter.
- Each sentence ends with the correct end mark.
- Each paragraph is indented.
- Each word is spelled correctly.

Proofreading Marks

∧ Add	≡ Capital letter
‿ Delete	/ Small letter
¶ Indent for new paragraph	

Using the Proofreading Marks

              dog
Sparky is a ~~doge~~. she is

Andy's pet.

3 **Review** these rules before you proofread.

Grammar and Spelling Connections

Nouns and Pronouns Use the correct pronoun when replacing one or more nouns.

> Dale **and** Clara **weren't home.**
>
> They **were at the park.**

Long Vowel Sounds The long **e** sound may be spelled e, ee, ea, or y.

> me   green   read   happy

📖   See the Spelling Guide on page H40.

▶ Publish Your Story

1 Make a neat final copy of your story.

2 Write an interesting title. Tell something about your story, but don't give away what happens.

- Be sure you wrote all letters correctly and used good spacing. Check that you fixed every mistake.

- Begin the first, last, and each important word in your title with a capital letter.

3 Look at Ideas for Sharing on the next page.

4 Publish or share your story in a way that works for your audience.

▶ Reflect

Answer these questions about your story.

- What is your favorite part of your story? Why?

 Do you like your story better than other papers you have written? Why or why not?

Tech Tip If you wrote your story on a computer, fix each mistake. Then print out a final copy.

Ideas for Sharing

Write It

- Bind your story with your classmates' stories to make a class book.
- Write your story as a play.

Say It

- ★ Read your story aloud while some classmates act it out.
- Tell your story to a classmate. Use your voice and body movements to make it more interesting.

> Change the tone of your voice as you read your story to make it sound more exciting.

Show It

- Make three paintings that show the beginning, middle, and end of your story.
- Present your story, using finger puppets.

Writing Prompts

Use these prompts for ideas or to practice for a test. Write your story in a way that your audience will understand and enjoy.

1 Write a story about a hero. What problem will the hero solve? How does the hero solve the problem?

2 What amazing place can you write about? What adventure could a character have there? Write a story about the adventure.

Writing Across the Curriculum

3 FINE ART

What is happening in this painting? Where and how did the boy get the deer? Write an interesting story about the boy and the deer.

Charles Scribner's Sons, Oil on canvas, 45 X 32 in. Private Collection
Photography by Peter Ralston

Jody and Flag, 1939, N.C. Wyeth
The Yearling, by Marjorie Kinnan Rawlings

See www.eduplace.com/kids/hme/ for more prompts.

✓ Test Practice

Read this writing prompt.

Write a story about a hero. What problem will the hero solve? How does the hero solve the problem?

Follow these steps for writing to a prompt.

① **Look** for clues that tell you what to write.

② **Look** for questions that you should answer.

③ **Plan** your writing. Copy and fill in this chart.

Answering a Writing Prompt
Clues: **a story about a hero; solve the problem**
Hero:
Problem:
Beginning:
Middle:
End:

④ **Look** at page 149. What makes a Superstar?

⑤ **Write** your story.

Writing a Book Report

In a **book report**, you write about a book you have read. You also tell if you liked the book and why. Read Celsey's book report and what W.R. said about it.

You wrote the **book title** and the **author's name**. Good!

> I'm Too Big/Je Suis Trop Gros
> by Lone Morton

I like the way you told **about the book**.

> This book is written in French and in English. It tells a story about an elephant and a giraffe who are unhappy. They are always trying to change the way they look.

Reading your **opinion** makes me want to read the book.

> My favorite part of the story is the ending. The elephant and the giraffe look at each other and really think that they're special just the way they are.
>
> Everyone should read books like this because they make you feel good about yourself and see that everyone is different. That is what makes everyone so special!

See www.eduplace.com/kids/hme/ for more examples of book reports.

- What is the **title** of the book that Celsey read?
- Who is the **author** of the book?
- What is this **book about**?
- What is Celsey's **opinion** of the book?

How to Write a Book Report

1 **Read** a book that interests you.

2 **Write** the book title and the author's name.

3 **Describe** what the book is about. Write about the main ideas.

Capitalize the first, last, and other important words in the book title. Draw a line under the title.

4 **Explain** your opinion.

- Tell if you liked the book or not. Then tell why.

- If the book has pictures, tell what you think of them. Did they add to the story? How?

5 **Proofread** your book report. Use the Proofreading Checklist on page 153. Use a class dictionary to check your spelling.

6 **Publish or share** your report. Read it aloud or display your final copy.

Different Forms of Stories

Some stories, like the one you just heard, have only words. When you read or hear them, you must create pictures of the characters and places in your mind.

Think and Discuss

What are the frog and rabbit like in this first set of pictures? What are they like in the second set? How do the pictures change your ideas about the setting and the characters in the story your teacher read?

You know that pictures can help you understand a story. They can show you what the weather is like and if a place is cheerful or gloomy. Pictures can also show you what a character looks like or how a character feels.

Music and other sounds can also help you understand a story. They can make a story seem sad, funny, calm, exciting, or even scary. Characters' voices can make them sound nice, mean, happy, or upset.

Apply It

Look at the picture on this book cover.

- What do you think this story might be about?

- Do you think it will be happy, sad, exciting, or scary? Why?

Now listen as your teacher plays some music that goes with this story.

- How did the music make you feel?

- Did the music make you change your mind about the story? Why or why not?

Verbs

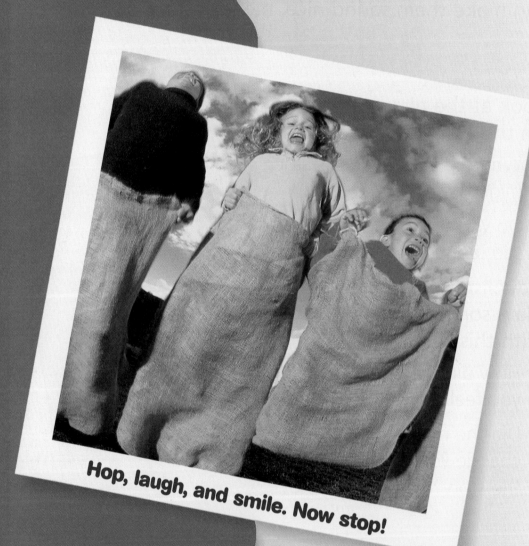

Hop, laugh, and smile. Now stop!

Verbs

Read the sentence. Which word tells what <u>it</u> does to the cool sand? What do you think <u>it</u> is? What can you do with or on sand?

It warms the cool sand.

—from <u>The Seashore Book</u>, by Charlotte Zolotow

A **verb** names an action that someone or something does or did. A verb is found in the action part of a sentence. What are the verbs in these sentences?

Alex **runs** beside the water.   She **played** in the sand.

Try It Out

Speak Up Say each sentence, using a verb from the Word Box.

| swim | dig | sails | blows |

1. The wind _____.   **3.** Fish _____.

2. A boat _____.

Write It Now write each sentence and draw a line under the verb.

Example Children _____ in the sand.

Children <u>dig</u> in the sand.

Write each sentence. Draw a line under the verb.

Example I make a sand house. I <u>make</u> a sand house.

1. I fill a pail.

2. I swim fast.

3. I eat lunch.

4. Birds fly by.

5–6. Look at Sam's photo album. Write the number of each photo. Next to the number, write the sentence that tells about the photo. Draw a line under the verb.

Example I find shells. I <u>find</u> shells.

- Girls wade in the water.
- Ron and I play in the sand.

5.

6.

Writing Wrap-Up WRITING • THINKING • LISTENING • SPEAKING

INFORMING

Write Picture Labels

Draw pictures of yourself doing different things. Write a sentence about each picture. Read your sentences to a classmate. Have the classmate say each verb.

For Extra Practice, see page 196.

2 Verbs That Tell About Now

Clap your hands as a classmate watches. Then clap together. For each action, say a sentence to tell what you are doing. Repeat with other actions.

Al claps.
Al and Jim clap.

A verb can name an action that is happening now. Add **s** to this kind of a verb when it tells about a noun that **names one**. Read the sentences. Which noun names one? Does the verb end with <u>s</u>?

A **girl** walk**s**.   The girls walk.

Try It Out

Speak Up Say each sentence, using the correct verb.

1. The girls (swing, swings) high.

2. Lee (run, runs) very fast.

3. Hannah (jump, jumps) down.

Write It Now write the sentences correctly.

Example Scott (slide, slides).
        Scott slides.

Choose and write the correct verb for each sentence.

Example The ball (roll, rolls) in the lake. rolls

1. A big dog (jump, jumps) into the water.

2. The dog (get, gets) the ball.

3. He (swim, swims) to shore.

4. The girls (thank, thanks) the wet dog.

5–8. Now copy the title and sentence below. Correctly write the sentences above to finish Lily's book summary.

Big Dog to the Rescue

The ball rolls in the lake.

_____

_____

_____

_____

Writing Wrap-Up

WRITING • THINKING • LISTENING • SPEAKING

SUMMARIZING

Write a Book Summary

Write sentences telling what happens in a book. Use verbs that tell about now. Read your summary to a classmate. Have the classmate name the verbs that tell about now.

   For Extra Practice, see page 197.

3 Pronouns and Verbs

Make up three sentences about the picture.
Use the words <u>they</u>, <u>it</u>, and <u>she</u>.

A **verb** can name an action that is happening now.
A **pronoun** can tell who or what is doing the action.
If the pronoun <u>he</u>, <u>she</u>, or <u>it</u> comes before a verb that
tells about now, add <u>s</u> or <u>es</u> to the verb.

She crack<u>s</u> the eggs.   **We crack** the eggs.

He mix<u>es</u> the eggs.   **You mix** the eggs.

Try It Out

Speak Up Say each sentence, using the correct verb.

1. I (get, gets) paint.

2. She (reach, reaches) for a hammer.

3. He (fix, fixes) the birdhouse.

4. It (look, looks) good.

Write It Now write
each sentence, using the
correct verb.

Example We (find, finds) some wood.

We find some wood.

Write each sentence, using the correct verb.

Example We (make, makes) a cake. We make a cake.

1. She (mix, mixes) the butter and the sugar.

2. I (add, adds) the milk and the eggs.

3–6. Proofread Carl's how-to list. Find four mistakes in using verbs with pronouns. Correct the verbs and write the list correctly.

Example I finds the berries. I find the berries.

How We Makes Fruit Salad

We brings four kinds of fruit.

You chop the fruit.

He mix everything together.

She serve the fruit salad.

Writing Wrap-Up   WRITING • THINKING • LISTENING • SPEAKING

NARRATING

Write a Story

Write about an adventure a boy, a girl, and some animals have. In some sentences use <u>he</u>, <u>she</u>, <u>it</u>, or <u>they</u> instead of nouns. Read your story. Have classmates name the pronouns and verbs.

4 Verbs with ed

Read the sentences. Which two words tell what Mac did?

Mac listened some more to the ocean sound. He smiled at the beautiful shell.

—from *Mac and Marie and the Train Toss Surprise*, by Elizabeth Fitzgerald Howard

Some verbs name actions that are happening now. Other verbs name actions that happened before now, or in the **past**. Add **ed** to most verbs to show that the action happened in the past.

We walk on the beach.

Yesterday we walk**ed** on the beach.

Try It Out

Speak Up Say each sentence, using the verb that names a past action.

1. Boats (rocked, rock) in the water.

2. Waves (wash, washed) the rocks.

Write It Now write the sentences.

Example We (watch, watched) birds.

We watched birds.

Write each sentence, using the verb that tells about the past.

Example We (look, looked) in the water.
We looked in the water.

1. We (discover, discovered) little fish.

2. Crabs (peeked, peek) out from rocks.

3. Seaweed (float, floated) by.

4. Justin (picked, pick) up a shell.

5–7. Copy Flora's journal entry. Change each verb in ( ) so that the sentences tell about the past.

Example My family (camps) _____ near the beach.
My family camped near the beach.

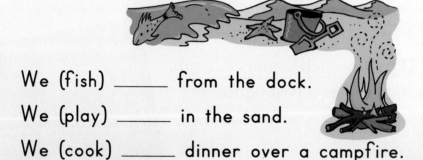

We (fish) _____ from the dock.

We (play) _____ in the sand.

We (cook) _____ dinner over a campfire.

![Writing Wrap-Up](WRITING • THINKING • LISTENING • SPEAKING)

EXPRESSING

Write a Journal Entry

Write about what you did yesterday. Use verbs that tell about the past. Read your sentences to a classmate. Have the classmate name the verbs. Compare what you did.

Combining Sentences: Action Parts

Joining Action Parts You may write two sentences that have the same naming part. Join them to make one longer sentence. Write the naming part. Then write the two **action parts** with <u>and</u> between them.

We **went on a walk**.

We **looked at plants**.

We **went on a walk** <u>and</u> **looked at plants**.

Try It Out

Speak Up/Write It Read the two sentences next to each number. Use <u>and</u> to join their action parts. Then say and write the new longer sentence.

Example   We took paper. We drew plants.
We took paper and drew plants.

1. Ann saw flowers.
   Ann smelled one.

2. I drew a fern.
   I colored it.

Revising Strategies continued

Apply It

1–9. Read this science report. Copy each pair of underlined sentences and circle the action parts. Then use <u>and</u> to join the action parts and make a longer sentence. Write each new sentence.

Example <u>Light gives plants energy.</u> <u>Light helps them grow.</u>

Light ⟨gives plants energy.⟩ Light ⟨helps them grow.⟩
Light gives plants energy and helps them grow.

Revising

Sasha and I did a test with two plants. <u>Sasha put her plant in a box.</u> <u>Sasha closed the top.</u> I left my plant out of the box.

<u>We watered our plants.</u> <u>We checked them each day.</u> In a week, our plants looked different. My plant was healthy. <u>Sasha's plant bent over.</u> <u>Sasha's plant had brown leaves.</u>

5 ran, run and came, come

What is wrong with the answer to this riddle?

How can you fix it?

Riddle Why did the clock lose the race?

Answer It run out of time.

The **helping verbs** <u>has</u> and <u>have</u> are used with <u>run</u> and <u>come</u> to tell about the past. <u>Has</u> and <u>have</u> are not used with <u>ran</u> and <u>came</u>. These **verbs** already tell about the past.

> Dad and Uncle Ed **came** to the race.
>
> They **have come** often.
>
> Uncle Ed **ran** on a team in school.
>
> He **has run** in many races.

Try It Out

Speak Up Say each sentence, using the correct verb.

1. A dog has (ran, run) after Amy.

2. Two kittens have (ran, run) after the dog.

3. Now the kittens have (came, come) back.

4. They (came, come) back a while ago.

Write It Now write the sentences correctly.

Example Amy (ran, run) to the barn. Amy ran to the barn.

Write each sentence, using the correct verb.

Example: The track team (come, came).

The track team came.

1. The coach has (came, come) too.

2. The boys (ran, run) last night.

3–5. Proofread this sports article. Find mistakes with three underlined verbs. Write the sports article correctly.

Example Sue <u>come</u> to the race last year.

Sue came to the race last year.

Proofreading

Big Race Won by Speedy Sue

Many people have <u>came</u> to the race today. Sue has <u>ran</u> in many races. Everyone ran fast. Sue <u>run</u> faster than anyone! She won the race.

Writing Wrap-Up WRITING • THINKING • LISTENING • SPEAKING

INFORMING

Write a Sports Article

Write an article about an animal race. Use the verbs <u>ran</u> and <u>came</u>. Use <u>has</u> or <u>have</u> with <u>run</u> and <u>come</u>. Read the article to a classmate. Work together to check that you have used verbs correctly.

6 saw, seen and went, gone

One-Minute Warm-Up

Read the sentence. Now say a new sentence about what you think Olly saw.

Instead of frogs he saw something he had never seen before.

—from Olly's Polliwogs, by Anne and Harlow Rockwell

The **helping verbs** <u>has</u> and <u>have</u> are used with <u>seen</u> and <u>gone</u> to tell about the past. <u>Has</u> and <u>have</u> are not used with <u>saw</u> and <u>went</u>. These **verbs** already tell about the past.

Grandpa and Jen **went** to the lake.

They **have gone** there many times.

Jen **saw** some frogs on the rocks.

She **has seen** them under rocks too.

Try It Out

Speak Up Say each sentence, using the correct verb.

1. Jen (saw, seen) two deer today.

2. The two deer have (went, gone) away.

3. They (went, gone) into the trees.

Write It Now write the sentences correctly.

Example Jen has (saw, seen) deer at the lake.

Jen has seen deer at the lake.

Write each sentence, using the correct verb.

Example We (went, gone) for a walk.

We went for a walk.

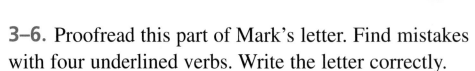

1. We (saw, seen) a skunk by a bush.

2. We have (seen, saw) skunks before.

3–6. Proofread this part of Mark's letter. Find mistakes with four underlined verbs. Write the letter correctly.

Example Dad <u>seen</u> beavers by the pond.

Dad saw beavers by the pond.

Dear Grandpa,

Dad and I have <u>went</u> to the pond many times. We have <u>saw</u> many birds there. Yesterday Dad <u>seen</u> two eagles. We went fishing and caught five fish. I <u>goed</u> right to bed when we got home!

WRITING • THINKING • LISTENING • SPEAKING

Writing Wrap-Up

DESCRIBING

Write a Letter

Write about a place you went and what you saw. Use <u>went</u> or <u>have gone</u> and <u>saw</u> or <u>have seen</u>. Read your letter aloud. Have a classmate listen to check that you have used verbs correctly.

7 did, done and gave, given

What is wrong with this sentence? How can you fix it?

I done this puzzle by myself.

The **helping verbs** <u>has</u> and <u>have</u> are used with <u>done</u> and <u>given</u> to tell about the past. <u>Has</u> and <u>have</u> are not used with <u>did</u> and <u>gave</u>. These **verbs** already tell about the past.

My grandmother **gave** us a puzzle.

She **has given** us many puzzles.

Matt and I **did** the puzzle.

We **have done** all of them.

Try It Out

Speak Up Say each sentence, using the correct verb.

1. A clown (did, done) a trick with balloons.

2. He has (did, done) the trick before.

3. He (gave, given) me two balloons.

4. I have (gave, given) one balloon away.

Write It Now write the sentences correctly.

Example A clown (did, done) a funny trick.

A clown did a funny trick.

Write each sentence, using the correct verb.

Example Inez (did, done) a painting. Inez did a painting.

1. Ted has (gave, given) a speech.

2. Julia and Pat (did, done) a play.

3–5. Proofread Ling's news article. Find mistakes with three underlined verbs. Write the article correctly.

Example Teachers <u>given</u> each class a job.
        Teachers gave each class a job.

Proofreading

School Clean Up

Mrs. Lee's class <u>done</u> posters about the clean up. A woman gave flowers to Mr. Johnson's class. The class planted a school garden. The children have <u>did</u> a good job. They have <u>gave</u> our school a wonderful gift.

Writing Wrap-Up WRITING • THINKING • LISTENING • SPEAKING

DESCRIBING

Write a Paragraph

Write about a job you have done. Use the verbs <u>gave</u> and <u>did</u>. Use <u>has</u> or <u>have</u> with <u>given</u> and <u>done</u>. Listen for these and other verbs when classmates read their paragraphs.

8 is and are

Answer these questions in complete sentences.

What animals are in line? Who is first in line? Who is next? Who is last?

The verbs <u>is</u> and <u>are</u> tell about something that is happening now. Use <u>is</u> if the sentence tells about **one** person, animal, place, or thing. Use <u>are</u> with nouns that name **more than one**. Read the sentences. Which tells about one? Which tells about more than one?

> **Jack** <u>is</u> in the race.
>
> **Marti and Bill** <u>are</u> also in the race.

Try It Out

Speak Up Say each sentence, using the correct verb.

1. The race (is, are) exciting.

2. Jack and Marti (is, are) fast.

3. People (is, are) cheering.

4. Jack (is, are) the winner.

Write It Now write the sentences correctly.

Example The children (is, are) ready to race.

The children are ready to race.

Write each sentence, using <u>is</u> or <u>are</u>.

Example My pet _____ a rabbit. My pet is a rabbit.

1. Her ears ____ long.   **2.** She ____ friendly.

3–6. Proofread these sentences from Dana's picture dictionary. Find four mistakes in using <u>is</u> and <u>are</u>. Write each sentence correctly and draw a picture.

Example S The sun are in the sky.
The sun is in the sky.

A Ants are small and black.
An apple are good to eat.

B A baby are wearing a bib.
Balloons is filled with air.

C Cats is good pets.
A clock is used to tell time.

Writing Wrap-Up WRITING • THINKING • LISTENING • SPEAKING

CREATING

Write Picture Dictionary Sentences

Think of four nouns that begin with the same letter. Write sentences about the nouns, using <u>is</u> and <u>are</u>. Listen for the correct use of <u>is</u> and <u>are</u> as classmates read their sentences.

9 was and were

One-Minute Warm-Up

Read the sentence. Read it again using <u>Danny and his friend</u> as the naming part. How does the sentence change?

Danny was in a hurry.

—from <u>Happy Birthday, Danny and the Dinosaur!</u>, by Syd Hoff

The verbs <u>was</u> and <u>were</u> tell about something that happened in the past. Use <u>was</u> if the sentence tells about **one** person, animal, place, or thing. Use <u>were</u> with nouns that name **more than one**. Which sentence tells about one? Which tells about more than one?

Paco's **birthday** <u>was</u> yesterday.

The **gifts** <u>were</u> a surprise!

Try It Out

Speak Up Say each sentence, using the correct verb.

1. The birthday party (was, were) at Paco's house.

2. Paco's friends (was, were) there.

3. The gifts (was, were) just what Paco wanted.

Write It Now write the sentences correctly.

Example The cake (was, were) good.

The cake was good.

Write each sentence, using <u>was</u> or <u>were</u>.

Example One gift _____ from Alma.

One gift was from Alma.

1. Two books _____ in a red box.

2. A new game _____ from Mother.

3–5. Proofread this thank-you note. Find three mistakes in using <u>was</u> and <u>were</u>. Write the thank-you note correctly.

Example My birthday were fun.

My birthday was fun.

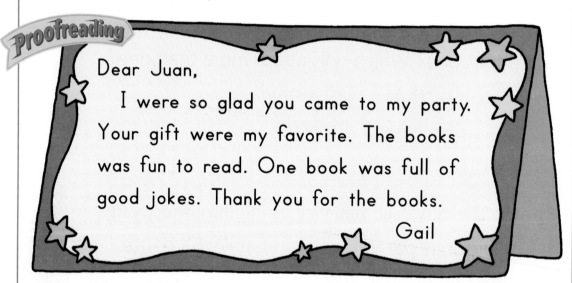

Proofreading

Dear Juan,

I were so glad you came to my party. Your gift were my favorite. The books was fun to read. One book was full of good jokes. Thank you for the books.

Gail

Writing Wrap-Up

WRITING • THINKING • LISTENING • SPEAKING

EXPRESSING

Write a Thank-You Note

Write a note thanking someone who gave you a gift or did something for you. Use <u>was</u> or <u>were</u>. Read your note aloud as classmates listen for the correct use of <u>was</u> and <u>were</u>.

10 Contractions

Say these two sentences. How are they different? How are they the same?

If it does not stop raining, we cannot go camping.

If it doesn't stop raining, we can't go camping.

A **contraction** is a short way of writing two words. An **apostrophe** (') shows where letters were left out.

do not	don't
does not	doesn't
is not	isn't
cannot	can't

Try It Out

Speak Up Say the contractions for these words. Use each contraction in a sentence.

1. does not   3. is not
2. cannot   4. do not

Write It Write the sentences, using a contraction for the underlined words.

Example This bird <u>is</u> <u>not</u> a pet. This bird isn't a pet.

5. Some birds <u>do</u> <u>not</u> fly south in winter.

6. An ostrich is a bird that <u>cannot</u> fly.

Write these sentences, using contractions for the underlined words.

Example <u>Do</u> <u>not</u> hike by yourself.
Don't hike by yourself.

1. Lindsay <u>does</u> <u>not</u> like camping.

2. Her tent <u>is</u> <u>not</u> new.

3–5. Proofread Sarika's story. Find three mistakes with contractions. Copy the story and write the contractions correctly.

Example Dont give up, Mrs. Small. Don't give up, Mrs. Small.

Proofreading

Mrs. Small cant find her new hat. She looks inside. She doesnt find her hat. She looks outside. Her hat is in a bird's nest! Mrs. Small isnt tall enough to reach it. She doesn't have a ladder. What will she do?

Writing Wrap-Up WRITING • THINKING • LISTENING • SPEAKING

NARRATING

Write a Story

Write about Mr. and Mrs. Nobody who are not willing or able to do things. Use <u>don't</u>, <u>doesn't</u>, <u>can't</u>, and <u>isn't</u>. Read your story. Have classmates name and spell the contractions.

Exact Verbs

Verbs are action words. When you write, use **exact verbs**. They make sentences come alive and tell your reader exactly what is happening.

The dogs <u>jump</u> for the ball.

The dogs **leap** for the ball.

Apply It

Writing Exact Verbs 1–5. Read this part of a science log. Copy the sentences and write an exact verb in place of each underlined verb. Use My First Thesaurus on page H45.

Example I <u>made</u> a cage for my hamster.

I built a cage for my hamster.

Our class has two new hamsters named Fluffy and Muffy. They <u>eat</u> the seeds we leave in their cage.

Fluffy <u>finds</u> a tube to run through. Muffy <u>jumps</u> on the wheel and makes it turn. Fluffy hides behind Muffy and <u>looks</u> at us. The hamsters make us <u>laugh</u>.

Enrichment

Verbs!

Contraction Match

Players	2
You Need	8 blank cards
Get Ready	Write <u>don't</u>, <u>doesn't</u>, <u>isn't</u>, and <u>can't</u> on four cards. Write the word or words that make each contraction on the other cards.

How to Play

Mix the cards. Put them face down in rows. Turn over two cards on each turn. Try to match a contraction with the word or words that make that contraction. For example, <u>don't</u> and <u>do</u> <u>not</u> are a match. If the cards match, keep them. If they do not match, turn them face down. The player with the most cards wins.

Flag Facts

• Draw and color the United States flag.

• Write two sentences about the flag. Use <u>is</u>, <u>are</u>, and verbs that show action.

Challenge Draw a school flag. Write sentences about it. Use <u>is</u>, <u>are</u>, and action verbs.

Verbs (page 163)

Write the sentences and draw a line under each verb.

1. The leaves fall from the trees.

2. Children jump in the leaves.

Verbs That Tell About Now (page 165)

Write each sentence, using the correct verb.

3. Children (play, plays) baseball.

4. Anna (throw, throws) the ball.

5. Jeff (swings, swing) the bat.

Pronouns and Verbs (page 167)

Write each sentence, using the correct verb.

6. I (hit, hits) the ball and run to first base.

7. He (catch, catches) the ball.

Verbs with ed (page 169)

Write each sentence, using the verb
that tells about the past.

8. Last night we (watch, watched) the sky.

9. We (looked, look) for falling stars.

10. Some clouds (cover, covered) the moon.

Special Verbs (pages 173, 175, 177)
Write each sentence, using the correct verb.

11. Jan (ran, run) home.

12. She has (came, come) from the fair.

13. She (saw, seen) the horses.

14. Tom (did, done) a trick with his pony.

15. They (gave, given) his pony a prize.

16. Jan has (saw, seen) Tom ride before.

is and are (page 179)
Write each sentence correctly.
Use is or are.

17. Grapes ＿＿ green.   18. A banana ＿＿ soft.

was and were (page 181)
Write each sentence correctly.
Use was or were.

19. The bike ＿＿ old.   20. The tires ＿＿ flat.

Contractions (page 183)
Write the contractions for these words.

21. is not   22. does not

Mixed Review

23–28. Proofread this letter. Find five mistakes with verbs and one mistake with a contraction. Write the letter correctly.

Proofreading Checklist

✔ Are came, went, and verbs that end in ed used to tell about the past?
✔ Is has/have used with given/done?
✔ Are was and were used correctly?
✔ Are contractions written correctly?
✔ Do verbs that tell about now and about one noun end with s?

Example The snails was moving slowly.
The snails were moving slowly.

Proofreading

Dear Kevin,

Uncle Max gave me a pet snail. I named it Speedy. Speedy live in a glass bowl. He doesn't move around much. Uncle Max owns a snail too!

Last night the two snails raced. They crawls on our racetrack. The race were very slow! Uncle Max's snail went only ten inches in one hour. Speedy done better. He crawled twenty inches. We have gave Speedy a little blue ribbon. I cant wait until the next race!

Becky

Test Practice ⭐

Number a sheet of paper from 1 to 6. Read each sentence. Choose the word that belongs in each space. Write the letter next to the correct answer.

1 Last week Pedro _____ the house.

   A painted

   B paint

   C paints

   D painting

2 Matt has _____ the dishes.

   F does

   G did

   H done

   J do

3 Last night Pat _____ sad.

   A are

   B is

   C were

   D was

4 Last month Scott _____ a TV show about whales.

   F saw

   G seen

   H see

   J sees

5 Dad has _____ me coins.

   A gave

   B give

   C given

   D gived

6 Pete _____ happy now.

   F are

   G is

   H was

   J were

Now write the numbers 7 to 12 on your paper. Read each sentence. Choose the word that belongs in each space. Write the letter next to the correct answer.

7 They have _____ to the store.

    A go

    B went

    C goed

    D gone

8 Yesterday two dogs _____ in our yard.

    F was

    G were

    H is

    J are

9 Now Sam _____ to open the door.

    A run

    B ran

    C runs

    D runned

10 I have _____ a rainbow in the sky.

    F seen

    G saw

    H see

    J sees

11 My best friend's birthday _____ last month.

    A was

    B were

    C is

    D are

12 Last week the twins _____ at my house.

    F plays

    G play

    H playing

    J played

Unit 1: The Sentence

What Is a Sentence? (pages 27–28)

Make sentences by matching the words in Box **A** with the words in Box **B**. Write the sentences.

A	**B**
1. The sun	eats a leaf.
2. The bug	sing in a tree.
3. Dad	shines brightly.
4. The birds	waters the garden.

Naming Part and Action Part (pages 29–32)

Write each sentence. Add your own naming part or action part to finish each one.

5. The girl _____.

6. _____ tastes good.

Is It a Sentence? (pages 33–34)

Write the complete sentence in each pair.

7. The letter was a surprise!
   A letter from Jill.

8. Fun to read.
   I answered it.

Which Kind of Sentence? (pages 37–46)

Write each sentence. Add the correct end mark. Tell if it is a telling sentence, question, command, or exclamation.

9. Do you like a circus

10. Please be quiet

11. I see the clowns

12. This is exciting

Unit 3: Nouns and Pronouns

Nouns (pages 93–96)

Write the sentences. Draw a line under each noun.

13. Was the lake warm?   14. A fly buzzed.

One and More Than One (pages 97–98, 101–104)

Write each noun to name more than one.

15. inch

16. woman

17. child

18. dog

Special Nouns (pages 105–106)

Write each sentence correctly. Use capital letters for special nouns.

19. I miss my friend doug.

20. He moved to denver.

Pronouns (pages 107–108)

Write each sentence, using a pronoun in place of the underlined word or words. Use <u>he</u>, <u>she</u>, <u>it</u>, or <u>they</u>.

21. <u>Carlos</u> hit the ball.

22. <u>The ball</u> went far.

Naming Yourself Last (pages 111–112)

Write the sentences correctly.

23. (James and I, I and James) ride bikes.

24. (Alma and me, Alma and I) play ball.

Nouns Ending with 's and s' (pages 113–116)

Write each word group. Does the first noun name one or more than one? Make this noun show ownership.

25. two birds nests   26. cat dish

Unit 5:   Verbs

Verbs (pages 163–164)

Write the sentences. Draw a line under each verb.

27. Darlene hides.   28. Jason finds her.

Verbs: Now and in the Past (pages 165–166, 169–170)

Write each sentence. Use the correct verb.

29. Ron (help, helps) clean the house.

30. Yesterday I (mow, mowed) the lawn.

Pronouns and Verbs (pages 167–168)

Write each sentence. Use the correct verb.

31. He (fixes, fix) the bike.

32. They (make, makes) lunch.

Special Verbs (pages 173–178)

Write each sentence. Use the correct verb.

33. Kim (ran, run) in the race yesterday.

34. Her family (come, came) to watch.

35. Juan has (gone, went) to a movie.

36. I have (saw, seen) many movies.

37. I (did, done) the jigsaw puzzle.

38. I have (gave, given) it to Cam.

is and are, was and were

(pages 179–182)

Write each sentence. Use the correct verb.

39. The circus (was, were) great.

40. The clowns (was, were) the best part.

41. The clowns (is, are) always funny.

42. My favorite clown (is, are) very tall.

Contractions (pages 183–184)

Write the sentences. Use a contraction for the underlined words.

43. He <u>is</u> <u>not</u> tall.

44. He <u>cannot</u> reach.

45. <u>Do</u> <u>not</u> fall.

(pages 163–164)

1 Verbs

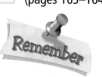

Remember

- A verb names an action that someone or something does or did.

●▲ Choose the verb from the Word Box that belongs in each sentence. Write the sentences.

| claps   toot   sings   plays |

Example The band _____ music.

The band plays music.

1. A girl _____ a song.

2. Two boys _____ horns.

3. The crowd _____ loudly.

■ **4–12.** Copy the box. Around the box, write each verb.

Example cut   sheep | Verbs | cut

chews	catch
dig	learn
sister	skips
read	first
run	crawl
swim	happy
teacher	sunny

| Verbs |

(pages 165–166)

2 Verbs That Tell About Now

- Add s to a verb that tells about one when the action is happening now. **Remember**

●▲ Write the correct verb for each sentence.

Example Josh (swim, swims). swims

1. Janet and Rachel (talk, talks).

2. Pedro (play, plays) baseball.

3. Chris (feed, feeds) his pet.

4. Doug and Dan (read, reads).

5. Kelsey (kick, kicks) a soccer ball.

■ Write each sentence. Use the correct verb.

Example Mom (make, makes) birdhouses.
Mom makes birdhouses.

6. Amy and Susie (help, helps) her.

7. Susie (paint, paints) the houses.

8. Amy (fill, fills) them with seeds.

(pages 167–168)

3 Pronouns and Verbs

Remember

- If the pronoun <u>he</u>, <u>she</u>, or <u>it</u> comes before a verb that tells about now, add <u>s</u> or <u>es</u> to the verb.

●▲ Write the correct sentence in each pair.

Example She like fruit. She likes fruit.
She likes fruit.

1. We shops for food.
   We shop for food.

2. He looks at the bread.
   He look at the bread.

3. It smells good.
   It smell good.

4. I wants some milk.
   I want some milk.

■ Write each sentence.
Use the correct verb.

Example She (drive, drives) a tractor.
She drives a tractor.

5. He (fix, fixes) the fence.

6. They (grow, grows) corn.

7. We (help, helps) pick corn.

(pages 169–170)

4 Verbs with ed

- Add ed to most verbs to show that the action happened in the past.

Remember

●▲ Write the sentences, using verbs that tell about the past.

Example Mother (starts, started) the car.
Mother started the car.

1. The car (turned, turns) left.

2. We (pass, passed) the school.

3. A school bus (honked, honks) at us.

■ Change each verb in ( ) so that the sentence tells about the past. Write the sentences correctly.

Example We _____ the car. (wash) We washed the car.

4. Dad _____ on the water. (turn)

5. John _____ the bucket. (fill)

6. Annie _____ some soap. (add)

7. I _____ the windows. (clean)

8. The car _____ great. (look)

5 <u>ran</u>, <u>run</u> and <u>came</u>, <u>come</u>

(pages 173–174)

Remember

- <u>Has</u> and <u>have</u> are helping verbs.
- Use these helping verbs with <u>run</u> and <u>come</u> to tell about the past.
- Do not use these helping verbs with <u>ran</u> and <u>came</u>.

●▲ Write each sentence. Use the correct verb.

Example They have (come, came) for the party.
They have come for the party.

1. Jesse (run, ran) all the way.

2. Evan (came, come) an hour ago.

3. Now Julie has (run, ran) to the door.

4. Ira has (came, come) with a big present.

■ Choose the correct verb from the Word Box to finish each sentence. Write the sentences.

| ran | run | came | come |

Example The team _____ on a bus.
The team came on a bus.

5. Maria's friend has _____ to the track meet.

6. Maria _____ in the relay race yesterday.

7. She has _____ in every race so far.

(pages 175–176)

6 **saw, seen** and **went, gone**

Remember

- **Has** and **have** are helping verbs.
- Use these helping verbs with **seen** and **gone** to tell about the past.
- Do not use these helping verbs with **saw** and **went**.

●▲ Write each sentence. Use the correct verb.

Example Nick (saw, seen) many frogs at the pond.

Nick saw many frogs at the pond.

1. He has (saw, seen) them there all summer.

2. Now summer has (went, gone).

3. Nick (went, gone) back to the pond today.

4. He (saw, seen) only a few frogs.

■ Choose the correct verb from the Word Box to finish each sentence. Write the sentences.

| saw |
| seen |
| went |
| gone |

Example Aunt Kim and I _____ on a whale watch.

Aunt Kim and I went on a whale watch.

5. Aunt Kim has _____ on one before.

6. She has _____ huge whales.

7. First we _____ a whale's tail.

8. Then the whale _____ under the ship.

(pages 177–178)

7 <u>did</u>, <u>done</u> and <u>gave</u>, <u>given</u>
- <u>Has</u> and <u>have</u> are helping verbs.
- Use these helping verbs with <u>done</u> and <u>given</u> to tell about the past.
- Do not use these helping verbs with <u>did</u> and <u>gave</u>.

Remember

●▲ Write each sentence. Use the correct verb.

Example Carlos (gave, given) Rosa a book on birds.
        Carlos gave Rosa a book on birds.

1. Rosa has (did, done) a report on birds.

2. She (gave, given) the report to her teacher.

3. Rosa has (did, done) a good job.

4. She (gave, given) the book to Sam.

■ Choose the correct verb from the Word Box to finish each sentence. Write the sentences.

did	done	gave	given

Example Dana _____ the prize to David.
        Dana gave the prize to David.

5. Mother has _____ us apples.

6. Lisa has _____ a math project.

7. Fran and I _____ cartwheels.

(pages 179–180)

8 is and are

- Is and are tell about something that is happening now.
- Use is to tell about one person, animal, place, or thing.
- Use are to tell about more than one.

Remember

●▲ Write each sentence. Use the correct verb.

Example The day (is, are) sunny.

The day is sunny.

1. The birds (is, are) singing.

2. Mother (are, is) picking flowers.

3. Dad (are, is) mowing the grass.

4. Rob and I (are, is) glad it is summer.

■ Use is or are to finish each sentence. Write the sentences correctly.

Example The zoo _____ full of animals.

The zoo is full of animals.

5. The baby elephant _____ wobbly.

6. The monkeys _____ funny.

7. The baby bears _____ cute.

8. The giraffe _____ tall.

9. The zookeeper _____ busy.

(pages 181–182)

⑨ was and were

- <u>Was</u> and <u>were</u> tell about something that happened in the past.
- Use <u>was</u> to tell about one person, animal, place, or thing.
- Use <u>were</u> to tell about more than one.

Remember

●▲ Write the correct verb for each sentence.

Example The boat (was, were) big. was

1. The sails (was, were) full of wind.

2. The wind (was, were) very strong.

3. White clouds (was, were) in the sky.

4. The sunshine (was, were) bright.

5. The waves (was, were) small.

■ Use <u>was</u> or <u>were</u> to finish each sentence. Write the sentences correctly.

Example Our hike _____ fun.
     Our hike was fun.

6. The path _____ narrow.

7. We _____ very high up.

8. Some hikers _____ tired.

Contractions

(pages 183–184)

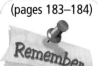
Remember

- A contraction is a short way of writing two words.
- An apostrophe (') shows where letters were left out.

●▲ Write each sentence, using a contraction
for the underlined word or words.

Example Dad <u>cannot</u> start the car.

Dad can't start the car.

1. It <u>does not</u> have any gas.

2. We <u>cannot</u> drive to school.

3. Buses <u>do not</u> come here.

4. It <u>is not</u> too far to walk.

■ Write each sentence, using the word or words that make
up the underlined contraction.

Example Ross <u>can't</u> go to school today.

Ross cannot go to school today.

5. Ross <u>doesn't</u> feel well.

6. He <u>isn't</u> getting out of bed.

7. I <u>don't</u> have any juice for him.

Writing Instructions

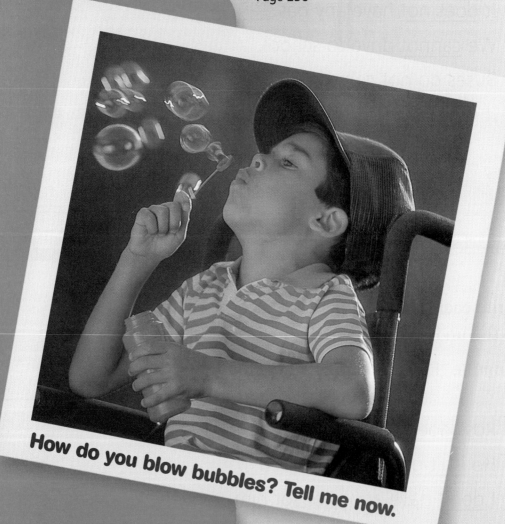

How do you blow bubbles? Tell me now.

Listening to Instructions

"Let's Make Rain" gives instructions for making rain in a plastic bag. What are the main steps?

Let's Make Rain

from the writers of Your Big Backyard

How would you like to make it rain? You'll need a sealable plastic bag, soil, grass, a spoon, water, a straw, and tape.

First, put a few spoonsful of soil in the bottom of the bag. Add a handful of grass. Pour a spoonful of water over the grass.

Next, place a straw at one end of the bag. Close the bag around the straw. Puff up the bag by blowing in the straw. Then have someone pull out the straw while you seal the bag.

Finally, tape the bag to a sunny window. After a while, you may see drops of water forming inside. When the drops get big enough they will roll down the sides. You've made rain in a bag!

Reading As a Writer

Think About the Instructions

- What are the main steps in making a bag of rain?

- What order words did the writer use?

- Which sentence first tells the topic of the instructions?

Think About Writer's Craft

- Why do you think the writer put the instructions in four paragraphs?

Think About the Picture

- Which step of the instructions does the picture above help you understand?

Responding

Write an answer to this question.

- **Personal Response** Would you enjoy making a bag of rain? Why or why not?

What Makes Great Instructions?

Instructions tell how to do something. Remember to do these things when you write instructions.

▶ Write about something that you know how to do well and can explain clearly.

▶ Begin with an interesting topic sentence.

▶ Write all of the steps in order.

▶ Make each step clear and complete.

▶ Use order words, such as <u>first</u>, <u>next</u>, <u>then</u>, and <u>finally</u>.

▶ Write an ending that will make your readers want to follow the instructions.

WORKING DRAFT

Read Matthew's instructions and what W.R. said.

Matthew Hodges

> I can tell that you really know about this topic.

> What could you say here to get your readers really excited about these instructions?

Here's how to grow a beautiful sunflower. You'll need a small shovel, a sunflower seed, and a sunny spot to plant it. First, ~~make~~ dig a hole that is two inches deep. Keep the dirt in one big pile to use later. Next, ~~cover the seed with dirt~~ drop the seed in the hole. Bury the seed with the dirt pile.

> What happens as the flower begins to grow?

Each morning when you wake up, water the place where you planted the sunflower seed. Finally, you will wake up and see a beautiful sunflower.

Reading As a Writer

- What changes might Matthew want to make?
- Why is it important to know what you need before you start to plant?
- Why did Matthew use <u>first</u>, <u>next</u>, and <u>finally</u>?

FINAL COPY

**Read Matthew's final copy
and what W.R. said about it.**

How to Grow a Sunflower
by Matthew Hodges

Growing sunflowers can be fun and easy.
Here's how to grow a beautiful sunflower.
You'll need a small shovel, a sunflower seed,
and a sunny spot to plant it.

First, use the shovel to dig a hole that
is two inches deep. Keep the dirt in one
big pile to use later. Next, drop the seed
in the hole. Then bury the seed with the
dirt pile and add some water.

Each morning when you wake up, water
the place where you planted the sunflower
seed. Soon a stem and leaves will begin to
grow. Finally, one day you will wake up
and see a beautiful sunflower.

> This topic sentence makes me want to keep reading.

> Good! You wrote all of the steps in order.

> Your ending makes me want to grow my own sunflower.

Reading As a Writer

- What did W.R. like about Matthew's final copy?
- What did Matthew add about planting the seed?
- Which sentence did Matthew add in the last paragraph? Why do you think he added it?

Write Instructions

▶ ## Choose Your Topic

1 **List** three things that you know how to do well.

2 **Tell** a classmate about each topic. Answer these questions.

- Which topic would your classmate like to learn about?

- Which topic can you explain best?

Stuck for an Idea?

How about these?

▶ something you have made

▶ a game you play well

▶ a special thing you can do

▶ something you do just for fun

See page 224 for more ideas.

3 **Copy and complete** these sentences. Name your audience and topic.

_____ will read or hear my instructions.

I will write about how to _____.

▶ Explore Your Topic

① **Look** at the pictures Matthew drew before he wrote. What other step could he have drawn?

1.

2.

3.

4.

② **Think** about your instructions.

③ **Draw** each step.

④ **Talk** with a classmate about your drawings. Explain each step. Is each step clear? Did you draw every step?

⑤ **Think** about your classmate's ideas. Change your drawings to make the steps clearer. Add drawings for any steps that you left out.

Focus Skill

Using Order Words

Order words make your instructions clear. Use order words like those in the box.

Order Words	
first	second
next	third
last	finally
then	now

Try It Together

Talk with your class about a game you play at school. Use order words to tell how to play.

▶ ## Think About Your Topic

1 **Look** at your drawings. Think about the order of the steps. Write an order word on each drawing.

2 **Make** an Order Chart like the one below. Write the order word from each drawing. Then write what the drawing shows.

Order Chart	
Order Word	**Step**

See www.eduplace.com/kids/hme/ for graphic organizers.

Focus Skill

Topic Sentence

A **topic sentence** tells the main idea of your instructions. Begin your instructions with a strong topic sentence.

Weak Topic Sentence	Strong Topic Sentence
Here's how to grow a beautiful sunflower.	Growing sunflowers can be fun and easy.
I like to draw.	Drawing animals is one of my favorite things.

Try It Together

Talk with your class about how to wash a dog. Together, write some good topic sentences.

▶ ## Plan Your Instructions

❶ **Write** two strong topic sentences for your instructions.

❷ **Mark** the one you like better.

▶ Write Your Instructions

Matthew used his Order Chart to help him write his instructions.

Order Chart	
Order Word	**Step**
first	Make a hole.

First, ~~make~~ dig a hole that is two inches deep.

1. **Copy** the topic sentence you marked onto another sheet of paper.

2. **Write** your instructions, using your Order Chart. Include details to make each step clear and complete.

3. **Write** an ending that will make your readers want to try your instructions.

In your instructions, use a comma after all order words except <u>then</u> and <u>now</u>.

How Good Are Your Instructions?

▶ **Copy** the sentences below that describe your draft.

Superstar

☐ I wrote an interesting topic sentence.

☐ I included all of the steps and wrote them in order.

☐ Each step is clear and complete.

☐ I used order words such as <u>first</u>, <u>next</u>, <u>then</u>, and <u>finally</u>.

☐ The ending will make readers want to try my instructions.

☐ My instructions have only a few mistakes.

Rising Star

☐ I need a more interesting topic sentence.

☐ Some steps are missing or are out of order.

☐ Some steps are unclear or are not complete.

☐ I could add some order words.

☐ I need to add an ending.

☐ My instructions have many mistakes.

See www.eduplace.com/kids/hme/ to interact with this rubric.

Unit 6: Instructions **217**

▶ Revise Your Instructions

❶ Look at the sentences from page 217 that you wrote about your instructions. What could you add or change to make your instructions better?

❷ Have a writing conference.

When You're the Writer

- Write a question about part of your instructions that you want help with.

- Share your instructions and your question with a classmate.

When You're the Listener

- Tell two things that you like about the instructions.

- Act out the steps. Ask questions about unclear or missing steps.

- Look on the next page for more ideas.

- Write a new topic sentence. Will it make your readers interested?

- Add order words.

- Make some steps clearer so they are easier for your audience to follow.

Tech Tip
If steps are out of order, use the Cut and Paste features to move them.

❸ Revise your instructions. Think about what you talked about with your classmate. Make changes to your draft. The Revising Strategies on page 220 may help you.

What to Say in a Writing Conference

If you are thinking . . .   You could say . . .

I don't know what the topic is.

What can you add to the beginning that tells exactly what you are writing about?

These steps are in the wrong order.

Are these steps in the correct order?

I don't understand how to do this step.

What details can you add to make this step easier to understand?

Revising Strategies

Word Choice Choose verbs that tell your readers exactly what to do.

> draw
> Then ~~make~~ a house.

▶ Draw a line under each verb in your instructions. Make two of them more exact.

📖 Use My First Thesaurus on page H45 to find exact verbs.

Sentence Fluency Two sentences may have the same naming part. Join them to make one longer sentence.

> and
> You pick the flowers, ~~You~~ put them in water.

▶ Try to find one place in your instructions where you can join two sentences that have the same naming part.

▶ Proofread Your Instructions

❶ Proofread your draft. Use the Proofreading Checklist and the Proofreading Marks.

❷ Use a class dictionary to check spellings.

Proofreading Checklist

☐ Each sentence has an action part.
☐ Each sentence begins with a capital letter.
☐ Each paragraph is indented.
☐ Each word is spelled correctly.

Proofreading Marks

∧ Add	≡ Capital letter
ℐ Delete	/ Small letter
¶ Indent for new paragraph	

Using the Proofreading Marks

put cereal in a B̸owl. Add
some
s̶u̶m̶ milk.

❸ Review these rules before you proofread.

Grammar and Spelling Connections

Complete Sentences Be sure each sentence has a verb.

First, find a yellow crayon.

Then draw a sun.

Long Vowel Sounds The long **i** sound may be spelled **y**, **igh**, or **i**-consonant-**e**.

try   might   like

📖 See the Spelling Guide on page H40.

▶ Publish Your Instructions

1 **Make** a neat final copy of your instructions.

2 **Write** an interesting title. Use words that tell exactly what you are writing about.

3 **Look** at Ideas for Sharing on the next page.

4 **Publish** or share your instructions in a way that works for your audience.

- Be sure you wrote all letters correctly and used good spacing. Check that you fixed every mistake.
- Begin the first, last, and each important word in your title with a capital letter.

▶ Reflect

Answer these questions about your instructions.

- What do you like most about your instructions?

- What do you like least about your instructions?

- What did you learn from writing your instructions?

 Do you like your instructions better than other papers you have written? Why or why not?

Tech Tip
If you wrote your instructions on a computer, fix all mistakes. Then print out a final copy.

Ideas for Sharing

Write It

- Write each step on an index card. Put the cards in order and number them.
- Bind your instructions with others written by your classmates to make a class book.

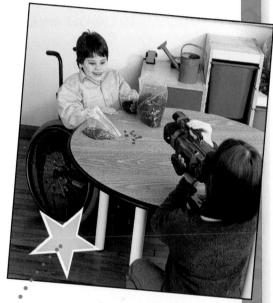

Say It

- Record your instructions so others can listen to the steps.
- Tell the steps in order while a friend tries to do them.

Look at the camera and speak clearly when you record your instructions.

Show It

- ★ Explain and demonstrate your instructions on videotape.
- Draw a poster to show the steps.

Tech Tip Use the shift key to make a capital letter for the first, last, and each important word in your title.

Writing Prompts

Use these prompts for ideas or to practice for a test. Write instructions that are easy to understand and follow. Include every step.

1 What are the steps in making a telephone call? Write instructions explaining each step.

2 How do you brush your teeth? Write instructions telling friends how to brush their teeth.

Writing Across the Curriculum

3 SOCIAL STUDIES

Write instructions that explain how to do one of your chores. Tell how to do each step.

4 ART

Write instructions that tell how to draw a house. Tell what you need and what you do first, next, and last.

5 PHYSICAL EDUCATION

Write instructions telling how to throw a basketball through a hoop. Tell where to stand and what to do with the ball.

6 MATH

Write instructions telling how to make a graph of the number of boys and girls in your class. Write the steps in order.

 See www.eduplace.com/kids/hme/ for more prompts.

Test Practice

On a test, you may be asked to write about a picture prompt. Read this prompt and look at the pictures.

Write instructions to go with the pictures below. Explain how to make a peanut butter sandwich.

Follow these steps for writing to a picture prompt.

❶ **Look** at each picture and answer these questions.

- What materials and steps are shown?
- How many steps are there?
- In what order are they shown?

❷ **Plan** your writing. Use an Order Chart like the one on page 214.

❸ **Look** at page 217. What makes a Superstar?

❹ **Write** your instructions.

Writing a Research Report

A **research report** gives facts about a topic. Read Candice's research report about giant pandas and what W.R. said about it.

Giant Pandas

> This is a good **opening**.

Giant pandas are mammals, just like dogs, cats, and people.

Giant pandas look like teddy bears. They are black and white. Some can be about five feet long, and they can weigh over two hundred pounds! Newborn giant pandas don't look special because they do not have black and white marks yet.

> You give many **details** to support the **main ideas**.

Giant pandas live in the mountain forests in China where there is bamboo for them to eat. Some giant pandas eat a huge amount of bamboo. Giant pandas will also eat plants, flowers, and even small animals. They can eat about thirty pounds of food in one day!

Giant pandas are endangered animals. Farmers cut down bamboo trees because they wanted to make room for farms. Many giant pandas died because they did not have bamboo to eat. Now people are trying to help the giant pandas survive. There are places called reserves where people are planting more bamboo for them. These are safe places for giant pandas.

Giant pandas look like black and white teddy bears. They live in the forests, but people in China are also making reserves where these endangered animals can eat bamboo and live safely.

> You summed up the main ideas in the **closing**. Great!

Sources

Schlein, Miriam. Jane Goodall's Animal World: Pandas. New York: Atheneum, 1989.

Snyder, Gregory K. "Panda." World Book Multimedia Encyclopedia. 1998 ed. CD-ROM. Chicago: World Book, Inc., 1998.

Reading As a Writer

- What interesting fact about giant pandas did Candice put in her **opening**?

- What is the **main idea** of Candice's third paragraph? What **details** support her main idea?

- What facts did Candice sum up in her **closing**?

How to Write a Research Report

1 **List** three topics that you would like to learn more about. Talk with a classmate about each topic. Answer these questions.

- Is this topic interesting enough?
- Can I find facts about this topic?

Stuck for a Topic?

How about these?
- ▶ an animal
- ▶ a famous person
- ▶ a famous place
- ▶ a sea creature
- ▶ a sport

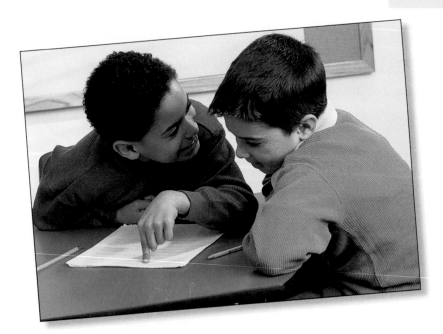

2 **Copy and complete** this sentence. Name your topic.

I will write about _____.

❸ Think of your report as a puzzle. Facts and details in a report are like the pieces that complete the puzzle. Look at the chart Candice used to help her explore facts and details about giant pandas.

Topic: Giant pandas		
What I Know	**What I Want to Learn**	**Where to Find Answers**
Giant pandas eat bamboo.	What else do they eat?	books about giant pandas, encyclopedia

Now make a chart like the one Candice used. Write what you know about your topic. Then write two questions you want to answer.

❹ Talk with your class about where you might find facts to answer your questions.

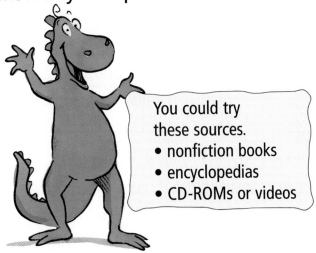

You could try these sources.
• nonfiction books
• encyclopedias
• CD-ROMs or videos

Beside each question in your chart, write two sources you will try. See Using the Library on pages H15–H16 for more tips.

Tech Tip
Before you use an Internet source, check with your teacher.

Include facts in a research report. Do not include opinions.

- A **fact** is something that is true or real. Giant pandas are animals.
- An **opinion** tells what someone believes or feels. Giant pandas are cute.

5 **Write** each question from your chart on a separate sheet of paper. Then read to find facts that answer your questions.

6 **Take notes** to remember the facts you find. Write only enough words to remember the information. Do not copy.

Read how one child took notes to answer this question. <u>Where do toucans live?</u> First, he found and read this information.

> If you cannot find the facts you need in one source, use another one.

> Toucans are birds found in the rain forests of Central and South America. They make their nests and sleep inside tree trunks.

Then he took these notes.

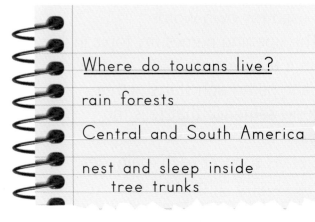

<u>Where do toucans live?</u>

rain forests

Central and South America

nest and sleep inside
    tree trunks

7 **Order** your notes. Number the questions from your chart in the order you will use them in your report.

Tech Tip
You can use a computer to record and organize your notes. See page H26.

8 **Draft** your report.

- Write an opening paragraph that names your topic in an interesting way.

- Next, write one paragraph to answer each of your questions. Rewrite each of your questions as a topic sentence. Use your notes to write the details. Use your own words.

- Then write a closing paragraph that sums up the main ideas.

9 **Look** at the checklist. What can you do to make your research report better?

Revising Checklist

- ☑ I used my own words.
- ☑ The opening names my topic in an interesting way.
- ☑ Each paragraph starts with a topic sentence that tells the main idea.
- ☑ Details support each main idea.
- ☑ My closing sums up the main ideas.

10 **Have** a writing conference. Take notes to remember your classmate's ideas.

What to Say in a Writing Conference

If you are thinking . . .

The opening is boring.

I don't know what this paragraph is about.

This part is confusing.

You could say . . .

Could you add an interesting fact here?

What is the main idea of this paragraph?

Do all of these details belong together?

⑪ **Revise** your report.

⑫ **Proofread** your report. Use the Proofreading Checklist on page 221. Use a class dictionary to check your spelling.

⑬ **Publish or share** your report.

Make a neat final copy, using your best handwriting.
Write a title for your report.
Include any pictures, maps, or charts.

● Read your report aloud or talk about it with a group. Show and explain your pictures.

★ Draw a report cover. Put your report in a classroom library for others to read.

Giving and Following Instructions

Giving Instructions

Have you ever told a friend or a younger child how to play a game or go from one place to another? If so, was it hard to do? Use these tips to give clear, easy-to-follow instructions.

Tips for Giving Instructions

▶ Tell what your instructions are about.
▶ Tell all of the important steps.
▶ Say the steps in the correct order.
▶ Use hand motions or other body movements.

Use Order Words

• First
• Next
• Then
• Finally

Then you kick the ball with the inside of your foot.

Apply It

Work with two classmates to plan instructions. Use order words and hand motions to explain how to walk from your classroom to another part of the school.

Listening to Instructions

Have you ever listened to instructions and then had to ask questions like these? Where do I put it? Which comes first? Use these tips to help you remember instructions and follow them correctly.

Tips for Listening to Instructions

▶ Give the speaker your full attention.
▶ Listen for details.
▶ Listen for order words.
▶ Watch for hand motions and other body movements.
▶ Retell the instructions.

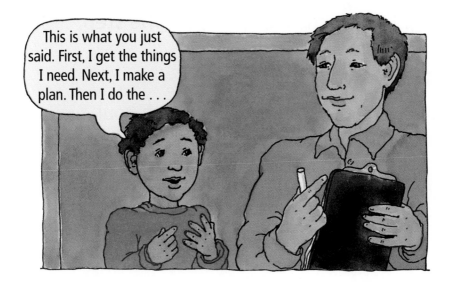

This is what you just said. First, I get the things I need. Next, I make a plan. Then I do the . . .

Apply It

Listen to the instructions that your teacher will say. Use the tips above to help you remember them. Then follow the instructions.

Following Picture Directions

Sometimes words are not needed to give directions. A picture or symbol can let you know what to do. Colors can also be used. Look at these examples. What does each picture mean?

A set of pictures can show you how to do or make something. Each picture shows you one step.

Try It Together

Talk about these picture directions with your class. What do they show you how to make? What do you need to make it? What details do you notice in each picture? Work with a classmate to follow the directions.

Tips for Following Picture Directions

▶ First, look over all the pictures.
▶ Then look for details in each one.
▶ Follow the steps in order.
▶ Finish the steps one at a time.
▶ Work slowly and carefully.

Follow these picture directions.

1

2

3

Adjectives

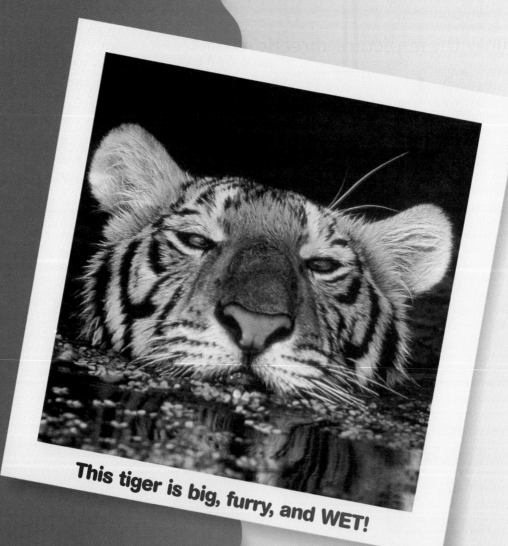

This tiger is big, furry, and WET!

Adjectives: How Things Look

One-Minute Warm-Up

Play I Spy. Think of a classroom object. Tell how it looks. Have classmates guess the object.

I spy something that is round and small.

A word that describes or tells how something looks is an adjective. **Adjectives** can tell size, color, shape, and how many. Say sentences, using the adjectives below.

Size	Color	Shape	How Many
big	red	round	three
small	gray	square	ten

Try It Out

Speak Up Say each sentence, using the correct adjective from the chart above.

1. Ben has _____ kittens. **(how many)**

2. He likes the _____ one best. **(color)**

3. Button is very _____. **(size)**

Write It Write the sentences correctly.

Example Button has a _____ face. **(shape)**

Button has a round face.

Finish each sentence with an adjective from the berry. Write the sentences.

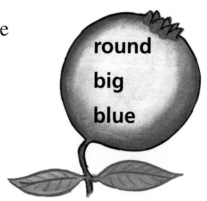

round
big
blue

Example The berry is _____. **(color)**

The berry is blue.

1. The berry is very _____. **(size)**

2. The berry is _____. **(shape)**

3–6. Copy Sid's poem. Draw lines under four adjectives.

Example The bugs are small. The bugs are <u>small</u>.

> Ladybugs
>
> Two bugs are on the sack.
>
> The bugs are red and black.
>
> The bugs are round with spots.
>
> I like the bugs a lot!

Writing Wrap-Up   WRITING • THINKING • LISTENING • SPEAKING

CREATING

Write a Poem

Write a poem. Use adjectives that tell size, shape, color, and how many. Try to make some lines rhyme. Read your poem. Have a classmate say the adjectives.

2 Adjectives: Taste and Smell

Read the sentence. Which word tells about kitchen smells?

Soon the kitchen fills with spicy smells.

—from Now We Can Have a Wedding! by Judy Cox

What other kind of smells might come from a kitchen?

Adjectives describe or tell how something looks. Adjectives also tell how something tastes and smells.

Taste		Smell
juicy ⟶	🍎 ⟵	sweet
sour ⟶	◉ ◉ ⟵	fresh

Try It Out

Speak Up Say each sentence, using the correct adjective from the Word Box below.

1. The corn tastes ____.

2. The toast smells ____.

3. The pickle tastes ____.

spicy	sour
sweet	burnt

Write It Now write the sentences correctly.

Example The stew smells ____. The stew smells spicy.

Write each sentence, using the correct adjective from the Word Box.

Example The forest smells _____.

The forest smells piney.

1. The peach tastes _____.

2. The fire smells _____.

smoky	sweet	piney

3–6. Read Carlota's journal entry. Copy the sentences. Circle the adjective that describes the underlined noun in each sentence.

Example I don't like sour <u>milk</u>. I don't like (sour) <u>milk</u>.

I like <u>roses</u> that smell sweet.

I don't like a <u>boat</u> that smells fishy.

I like to eat juicy <u>plums</u>.

I don't like burnt <u>toast</u>.

Writing Wrap-Up   WRITING • THINKING • LISTENING • SPEAKING

DESCRIBING

Write a Journal Entry

Describe foods you like and don't like. Use some adjectives that tell how each one tastes and smells. Read your entry. Have classmates name the adjectives you used.

3 Adjectives: Sound and Texture

Make a clapping sound and a clicking sound. What other kinds of sounds can you make? Now touch an object in your desk. How does it feel?

Adjectives describe how something looks, tastes, and smells. They also tell how something sounds and how it feels if you touch it.

The man has a **loud** voice.　　The cat's fur is **soft**.

Try It Out

Speak Up Say each sentence, using the best adjective from the Word Box.

barking	hard	crunching	wet

1. My cat's fur feels _____ from the snow.
2. The _____ dog slides on the ice.
3. This rock feels _____.

Write It Now write the sentences correctly.

Example I hear a _____ sound in the snow.

I hear a crunching sound in the snow.

Write each sentence, using the correct adjective from the Word Box.

loud

hot

fuzzy

Example The sun feels _____.

The sun feels hot.

1. We hear a _____ meow.

2. I pet the kitten's _____ fur.

3–5. Copy Lisa's riddles. Draw a line under the adjective in each sentence that tells how something sounds or feels. Then write the answer to each riddle.

Example What animal makes a squeaking noise? a mouse

3. What has wheels and makes a honking sound?

4. What feels sharp and is used with a hammer?

5. What feels sticky and bees make it?

WRITING • THINKING • LISTENING • SPEAKING

Writing Wrap-Up

CREATING

Write a Riddle

Write a riddle that describes something. Include how it sounds or feels. Read your riddle aloud. Have classmates name the adjectives and guess the answer.

Expanding Sentences: Adjectives

Using Adjectives to Tell More You may use **adjectives** to tell more about the nouns in your sentences. Use adjectives in your writing to make your sentences clearer and more interesting.

Hold my turtle.   Hold my **spotted** turtle.

Try It Out

Speak Up Read the sentences under the pictures. Use an adjective from the Word Box to tell more about each animal. Say the new sentences.

huge	silver
orange	colorful

1.

This ____ kitty needs a hug!

2.

The ____ fish swim fast!

3.

This ____ parrot talks.

Write It **1–3.** Now write the new sentences. Draw a line under each adjective.

Example The ____ lizard eats bugs.

The huge lizard eats bugs.

Revising Strategies continued

Apply It

1–4. Copy this book summary. Write an adjective from the Word Box before each underlined noun to tell more about it.

dark	green
young	grassy
noisy	

Example My pet is a <u>frog</u>.

My pet is a green frog.

Revising

Jay is a <u>boy</u>. He finds a cricket in a <u>field</u>. Jay keeps the cricket as a pet.

The cricket chirps in <u>places</u>. Jay brings his <u>pet</u> to school. The cricket chirps in Jay's pocket. The teacher lets Jay show everyone his new pet.

4 Using <u>a</u> and <u>an</u>

What might you find in your attic? With a classmate, take turns saying sentences like those on the chart. Use words that name one and say them in ABC order.

In my attic, I found an **anchor**.

In my attic, I found a **basket**.

The words **a** and **an** are **special adjectives**. Use these special adjectives before nouns that name one.

Use **a** before a noun that begins with a <u>consonant</u> <u>sound</u>. He had **a** <u>j</u>ob.

Use **an** before a noun that begins with a <u>vowel</u> <u>sound</u>. He cleaned out **an** <u>a</u>ttic.

Try It Out

Speak Up Say each group of words, using the correct word in ( ).

1. (a, an) bowl
2. (a, an) apron
3. (a, an) apple
4. (a, an) pie

Write It Now write each group of words correctly.

Example (a, an) table a table

Write the sentences, using <u>a</u> or <u>an</u> correctly.

Example (A, An) toy store has a sale.

         A toy store has a sale.

1. Nate buys (a, an) airplane

2. Kim wants (a, an) teddy bear.

3–6. Proofread Jake's poster. Find four mistakes in using <u>a</u> and <u>an</u>. Write the poster correctly.

Example Jake made an poster for the yard sale.

         Jake made a poster for the yard sale.

Come to a Yard Sale Today!

We have a umbrella and a bike.

Choose an toy to take home.

Get an glass of juice and a apple.

Write Sentences for a Poster

WRITING • THINKING • LISTENING • SPEAKING

INFORMING

Write three sentences for a poster that tells about an event or a sale. Use <u>a</u> and <u>an</u>. Show and read all of the posters. Together, make a class list of words used with <u>a</u> and <u>an</u>.

5 Adjectives with er and est

Look at the caterpillars. Say sentences that tell about their lengths.

Add **er** to adjectives to **compare two** people, animals, places, or things. Add **est** to **compare more than two** people, animals, places, or things.

short

short**er**

short**est**

Try It Out

Speak Up Say each sentence, using the correct adjective.

1. Beth is (taller, tallest) than Jan.

2. Nina is the (taller, tallest) girl of all.

Write It Write the sentences correctly.

Example Nina is (taller, tallest) than Beth.
Nina is taller than Beth.

Write each sentence, using the correct adjective.

Example A rabbit has (longer, longest) ears than a cat.

A rabbit has longer ears than a cat.

1. A horse is (faster, fastest) than a dog.

2. The blue whale is the (larger, largest) animal of all.

3–5. Proofread Miguel's notes. Find three mistakes in using <u>er</u> and <u>est</u>. Write each animal fact correctly.

Example A duck is smallest than a turkey.

A duck is smaller than a turkey.

Proofreading

Animal Facts

For short distances, a cheetah is

the faster animal of all.

A camel is tallest than a dog.

A swordfish is faster than a blue shark.

A giraffe is the taller animal.

Writing Wrap-Up WRITING • THINKING • LISTENING • SPEAKING

COMPARING & CONTRASTING

Write Animal Facts

Compare three animals. Use some adjectives that end in <u>er</u> and <u>est</u>. Read your sentences. Have a classmate name the adjectives you used. Draw pictures to go with your facts.

Combining Sentences: Adjectives

Joining Sentences with Adjectives You may write two sentences with **adjectives** that tell about the same noun. Join the two sentences, using <u>and</u> between the two adjectives. This will make your writing better.

The lizard is **large.**

The lizard is **scaly.**

The lizard is **large** <u>and</u> **scaly.**

Try It Out

Speak Up/Write It Read the two sentences under each picture. Join the sentences, using <u>and</u> between the two adjectives. Say and write each new sentence.

Example   A bat is small. A bat is furry.

A bat is small and furry.

1.

A turtle's shell is large.

A turtle's shell is hard.

2.

A manatee is big.

A manatee is friendly.

Revising Strategies continued

Apply It

1–3. Read this part of a class report about a zoo trip. Copy the underlined sentences and circle the two adjectives. Join the two sentences, using **and** between the two adjectives. Then write the new sentence.

Example   We saw animals that were (large).
We saw animals that were (scary).
We saw animals that were large and scary.

Revising

We saw a lion that was beautiful. We saw a lion that was proud. The lion was with her cub.

4–6. Now read the rest of the report. Copy the underlined sentences and circle the two adjectives. Join the two sentences, using **and** between the two adjectives. Then write the new sentence.

Revising

The lion walked through the tall grass. The cub let out a roar that was loud. The cub let out a roar that was fierce. Then the lion went back to her cub.

Antonyms

Words whose meanings are as different as they can be are called **antonyms** or **opposites**. Look at the pictures and read the sentence.

I can see that the **sad** girl is **happy** again.

Apply It

Writing Antonyms 1–3. Read and copy this journal entry. Finish each sentence with an antonym from the box that is the opposite of each underlined adjective.

Adjectives	Antonyms
shortest	tallest, longest
large	small, little
smooth	uneven, rough
light	heavy, dark

Example Ben has <u>smooth</u> stones, and Callie has _____ stones.
Ben has smooth stones, and Callie has rough stones.

Today we went hiking. We saw a <u>large</u> oak tree with a _____ pine tree at its base. Beth carried a <u>light</u> box of leaves, and Alex filled a box with _____ rocks for our campfire. Some of us took the <u>shortest</u> trail, but others took the _____ trail.

Enrichment

Pet Poems

- Read this poem. What adjectives describe the noun <u>dogs</u>?

- Write your own poem about another pet, using this one as a model.

- Change the kind of pet and the adjectives.

- Draw a picture of your poem.

Challenge Make a book of poems describing other animals.

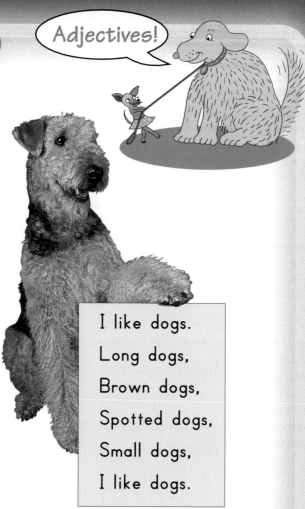

Adjectives!

I like dogs.
Long dogs,
Brown dogs,
Spotted dogs,
Small dogs,
I like dogs.

What is big, brown, and furry?

Riddle Roundup

- Write a riddle about an animal or thing. Use three adjectives to describe it. Draw the answer on the back.

- Trade riddles with classmates. Guess the answers.

Adjectives: How Things Look (page 239)

Choose the correct adjective from the Word Box to finish each sentence. Use the words in ( ) to help you.
Write the sentences.

1. There are _____ baby birds. **(how many)**

2. They live in a _____ nest. **(shape)**

3. They are _____ birds. **(size)**

4. They have _____ feathers. **(color)**

round
yellow
four
tiny

Adjectives: Taste and Smell (page 241)

Write the sentences. Circle the adjective that describes each underlined noun.

5. The <u>soap</u> smells flowery.

6. The <u>cheese</u> tastes creamy.

7. I like spicy <u>chili</u>.

8. I threw away the sour <u>milk</u>.

9. The <u>clams</u> taste fishy.

10. The <u>room</u> smells smoky.

Adjectives: Sound and Texture (page 243)

Write each sentence, using the correct adjective from the Word Box.

11. Glue is _____ to touch.

12. The playground sounds _____.

13. The old door is _____.

14. The egg feels _____.

creaky
noisy
sticky
smooth

Using a and an (page 247)

Write each group of words, using a or an correctly.

15. (a, an) girl

16. (a, an) ox

17. (a, an) clown

18. (a, an) eel

19. (a, an) man

20. (a, an) insect

Adjectives with er and est (page 249)

Write each sentence. Use the correct adjective.

21. Terry is (older, oldest) than John.

22. Which of the three girls has the (longer, longest) hair?

23. John's hair is (darker, darkest) than my hair.

24. Ann is (shorter, shortest) than Amy.

Mixed Review

25–30. Proofread this riddle. Find three mistakes with <u>a</u> and <u>an</u> and three mistakes with adjectives that compare. Write the riddle correctly.

Proofreading Checklist

✔ Is <u>a</u> used before a noun that begins with a consonant sound?

✔ Is <u>an</u> used before a noun that begins with a vowel sound?

✔ Are adjectives ending with <u>er</u> used to compare two people, animals, places, or things?

✔ Are adjectives ending with <u>est</u> used to compare more than two people, animals, places, or things?

Example Here is an riddle for you to solve.

Here is a riddle for you to solve.

Proofreading

I am an animal.

I am the bigger animal on earth!

I weigh more than an elephant.

I am longest than a school bus.

I live in a ocean, but I am not a fish.

I breathe through an hole on top of my head.

I eat tiny sea creatures called krill.

Krill are smallest than your finger.

I can eat thirty million krill in an day!

What am I?

Answer: I am a blue whale!

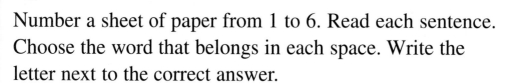

Test Practice

Number a sheet of paper from 1 to 6. Read each sentence. Choose the word that belongs in each space. Write the letter next to the correct answer.

1 Pam went to a pet shop. _____ saw many animals.

A They

B She

C He

D It

2 The striped fish is the _____ of all the fish.

F larger

G largest

H most large

J large

3 The gray kitten is _____ than the white kitten.

A fat

B more fat

C fattest

D fatter

4 A man fed the dog. _____ gave the dog a big bone.

F He

G She

H They

J It

5 The puppy played with a _____ ball.

A smaller

B more small

C smallest

D small

6 Kara and Ron buy fish. _____ buy six fish.

F She

G He

H They

J It

Now write the numbers 7 to 12 on your paper. Read each sentence. Choose the word that belongs in each space. Write the letter next to the correct answer.

7 Jim and Li are at the zoo. _____ like the zoo.

   A He

   B They

   C She

   D It

8 A baby giraffe is _____ than a baby lion.

   F tall

   G tallest

   H taller

   J more tall

9 A boa is the _____ of all the snakes at the zoo.

   A longer

   B most long

   C long

   D longest

10 A bear eats a juicy apple. _____ tastes good.

   F It

   G She

   H He

   J They

11 A man paints a picture. _____ paints the tigers.

   A They

   B He

   C She

   D It

12 Today seems like the _____ day of year!

   F hot

   G hotter

   H hottest

   J most hot

Now write the numbers 13 and 14 on your paper. Read the paragraph and find the numbered, underlined parts. The underlined parts may be one of the following:

- Groups of words that are not sentences
- Correctly written sentences that should be combined
- Correctly written sentences

Choose the best way to write each underlined part. Write the letter that is next to the correct answer. If the underlined part needs no change, write the letter next to "No mistake."

My family went to a beach. <u>Ben jumped into the cold water.</u>
(13)
<u>Ben jumped into the salty water.</u> He splashed in the waves.

Later Ben and I played in the sand and looked for shells. The

shells were hard and white. We filled a big pail with shells.

<u>We ate lunch. On the beach.</u>
(14)

---

13 A Ben jumped. Into the cold and salty water.

B Ben jumped into the cold water. The salty water.

C Ben jumped into the cold and salty water.

D No mistake

14 F We ate lunch on the beach.

G We ate. lunch on the beach.

H We ate lunch on the beach?

J No mistake

(pages 239–240)

1 **Adjectives: How Things Look**

- A word that describes how something looks is an adjective.
- Adjectives can tell size, color, shape, and how many.

Remember

●▲ Write each sentence, using an adjective from the Word Box. Look at the word in ( ) for help.

large	green
round	one

Example The store sold _____ beach ball today. **(how many)**
The store sold one beach ball today.

1. The beach balls are _____. **(shape)**

2. This one is very _____. **(size)**

3. It has big _____ dots. **(color)**

■ Write the sentences. Draw a line under each adjective.

Example The toys are small. **(size)**
The toys are <u>small</u>.

4. I have three cars. **(how many)**

5. I like the blue car best. **(color)**

6. The tires are big. **(size)**

7. The windows are square. **(shape)**

8. It has four doors. **(how many)**

9. The red car has a stripe on it. **(color)**

10. The stripe is thin. **(size)**

(pages 241–242)

2 Adjectives: Taste and Smell

- Adjectives can tell how something tastes and smells.

Remember

●▲ Choose an adjective from the Word Box to finish each sentence. Write the sentences.

| sweet | spicy | stale | smoky |

Example The perfume smells _____.

The perfume smells sweet.

1. The old crackers taste _____.

2. Our campfire smells _____.

3. Many Mexican foods taste _____.

■ Write the sentences. In each sentence, circle the adjective that describes the underlined word.

Example The <u>stew</u> tastes peppery. The <u>stew</u> tastes (peppery.)

4. The <u>wash</u> smells soapy.

5. The <u>milk</u> tastes sour.

6. The <u>ice cream</u> tastes minty.

7. The <u>woods</u> smell piney.

8. The <u>roses</u> smell sweet.

(pages 243–244)

Remember

3 Adjectives: Sound and Texture

- Adjectives can tell how something sounds and how it feels when you touch it.

●▲ Choose an adjective from the Word Box to finish each sentence. Write the sentences.

| cool | hot | loud | soft |

Example The sun feels _____.

The sun feels hot.

1. A whisper sounds _____.

2. The shade feels _____.

3. The horn sounds _____.

■ Write the sentences.
Draw a line under each adjective.

Example The grass feels wet.

The grass feels <u>wet</u>.

4. The band plays loud music.

5. I sit on the soft blanket.

6. The breeze feels cool on my face.

7. I am wearing a silky dress.

8. I hear a buzzing bee.

(pages 247–248)

Remember

4 Using a and an
- Use **a** and **an** before words that name one.
- Use **a** before words that begin with a consonant sound.
- Use **an** before words that begin with a vowel sound.

●▲ Choose the correct word in ( ). Write each group of words.

Example (a, an) ox an ox

1. (a, an) cookie

2. (a, an) egg

3. (a, an) apple

4. (a, an) pear

5. (a, an) frog

6. (a, an) otter

7. (a, an) hen

8. (a, an) elephant

■ Write each sentence, using **a** or **an** correctly.

Example I can ride _____ horse.
    I can ride a horse.

9. Can you find _____ ant on the flower?

10. That animal covered with mud is _____ pig!

11. I see _____ inchworm on a leaf.

12. Where does _____ bear live?

(pages 249–250)

5 **Adjectives with er and est**

Remember

- Add <u>er</u> to adjectives to compare two people, animals, places, or things.
- Add <u>est</u> to adjectives to compare more than two.

● ▲ Choose the correct adjective for each sentence. Write the sentences.

Example Is my room (smallest, smaller) than your room?

Is my room smaller than your room?

1. The bookcase is (taller, tallest) than the door.

2. This is the (stronger, strongest) chair of all.

3. Which is the (shorter, shortest) book of the four?

4. The wall is (cleanest, cleaner) than the floor.

■ Add <u>er</u> or <u>est</u> to each adjective in ( ). Write the sentences correctly.

Example Jim is (short) than Sue.

Jim is shorter than Sue.

5. Spot is the (old) pet of the four.

6. Inez has (long) hair than Anna.

7. Lee is (young) than Tom.

Writing a Description

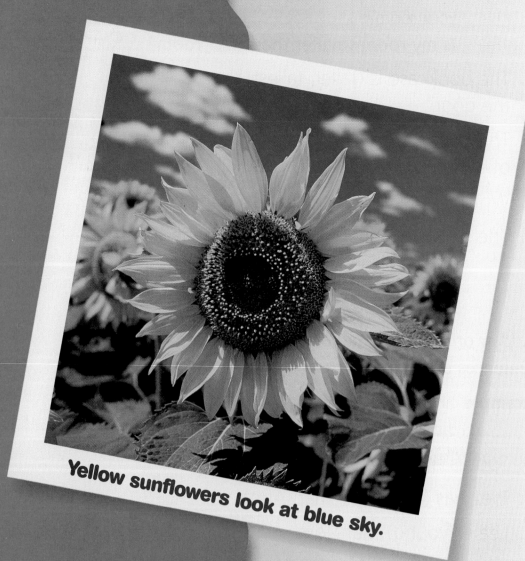

Yellow sunflowers look at blue sky.

Listening to a Description

"The Fog Rolls In" describes what people do as the weather changes in a beach town. What sensory words does the writer use to help you feel and see what is happening?

The Fog Rolls In

from Hide and Seek Fog, by Alvin Tresselt

On the beach, the sand was suddenly cold and sticky. The mothers and fathers gathered up blankets and picnic baskets. They called — "Cathy! John! Come out of the water! We're going now!"

See www.eduplace.com/kids/
for information about Alvin Tresselt.

Unit 8: Description   **267**

The children ran in and out one more time, blue-lipped and shivering. They scurried about looking for lost pails and shovels. They scooped up one more pretty shell and a gray seagull feather. Then everyone trudged across the chilly sand and cold rocks back to cars and cottages.

The lobsterman delivered his lobsters to the fishing wharf. He hurried home through winding streets, just as the fog began to hide the town.

The sailboats bobbled like corks on the dull gray water of the cove. Their sails were wrapped for the night, and the sailors rowed through the misty fog back to land.

But indoors in the seaside cottages the children toasted marshmallows over a driftwood fire, while the fog tip-toed past the windows and across the porch.

Reading As a Writer

Think About the Description

- What sensory words does the writer use to help you feel and see what is happening?

- Which words on page 269 tell how the fog moved past the houses?

Think About Writer's Craft

- What does the writer compare the sailboats to? How are the two things alike?

Think About the Pictures

- Look at the pictures on pages 268 and 269. Which picture shows the fog? How do you know?

Responding

Write an answer to this question.

- **Personal Response** What part of the description did you enjoy most? Why?

What Makes a Great Description?

A **description** helps your readers see, feel, hear, taste, and smell what you are writing about. When you write a description, remember to do these things.

▶ Describe one thing, place, or event.

▶ Begin with a clear and interesting topic sentence that tells what you will describe.

▶ Use your senses to get information about your topic. Use sensory words to write about it.

▶ Use exact words and details.

▶ Use words that compare or tell how your topic is like something else.

GRAMMAR CHECK

Use the endings <u>er</u> and <u>est</u> correctly with adjectives.

Christine Guzman

WORKING DRAFT

Read Christine's description and what W.R. said about it.

> I like the way you tell how the pool is like a peanut.

I like my grandmother's new swimming pool. It is shaped like a fat peanut. The pool is built-in, and it is about ten feet deep. ~~My brother and I always~~ If you look inside it, you see that the bottom of the pool is light blue. The stairs are light blue too. The sides are white, and so is the diving board.

> What can you compare the cold water to?

When you dive into the pool, it feels cold. You can put ~~cold~~ freezing water on your body first and then jump into the pool. Then the pool feels very, very warm. If you jump in the pool from the diving board, it makes a splashing sound. I wish I could swim there every day.

> Freezing is a good sensory word!

Reading As a Writer

- What one thing did Christine describe?
- What can Christine add to help her readers hear the splashing sound?

FINAL COPY

Read Christine's final copy
and what W.R. said about it.

My Grandmother's Pool
by Christine Guzman

My grandmother's new swimming pool is
great! It is shaped like a fat peanut. The
pool is built-in, and it is about ten feet deep.
If you look inside it, you see that the bottom
of the pool and the stairs are light blue. The
sides are white, and so is the diving board.

When you dive into the pool, it feels like
you are jumping into a giant, ice-cold glass
of water. You can put freezing water on
your body first and then jump into the pool.
Then the pool feels very, very warm. If you
jump in the pool from the diving board, it
makes a sound like one hundred firecrackers.
I wish I could swim there every day.

> This topic sentence makes me want to read more.

> I like the way you describe the outside of the pool and then the inside.

> This detail helps me hear exactly what jumping in from the diving board sounds like.

Reading As a Writer

- What adjective did Christine use in her first sentence to make it better?
- What details did Christine add to help her readers see, hear, and feel what the pool is like?

 See www.eduplace.com/kids/hme/ for more examples of student writing.

Unit 8: Description

273

Write a Description

▶ **Choose Your Topic**

1 **List** three things that you could describe.

HELP ? **Stuck for an Idea?**

How about these?
- ▶ your favorite toy
- ▶ your bedroom
- ▶ a pet
- ▶ your favorite food

See page 286 for more ideas.

2 **Share** and talk about each of your ideas with a classmate. Answer these questions.

- Which idea does your classmate think is the most interesting?

- Which topic can you describe best?

3 **Copy and complete** these sentences. Name your audience and topic.

_____ will read or hear my description.

I will describe _____.

Focus Skill

Using Your Senses

You use your five senses to taste, smell, touch, hear, and see. Gather details about your topic, using your senses.

Try It Together

How does your classroom look, sound, and smell? With your class, make a list of adjectives that describe your classroom.

Explore Your Topic

❶ **Think** about your topic.

❷ **Make** a chart like the one below. Write details about your topic. Describe what you observe, using your senses. List details for at least three senses.

Five Senses Chart				
My Topic:				
See	Hear	Touch	Taste	Smell

See www.eduplace.com/kids/hme/ for graphic organizers.

▶ Plan Your Description

You can organize your details in many ways. Christine used a word web to organize the details from her Five Senses Chart. She wrote details telling what the pool is like from the outside and from the inside.

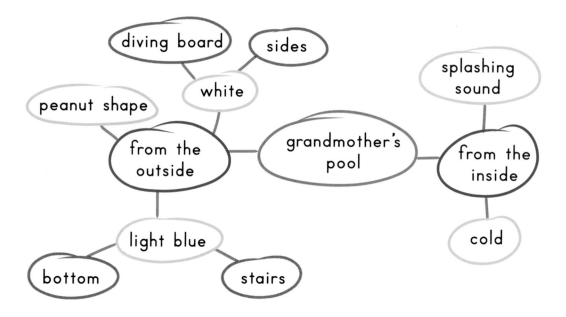

1 **Think** about your topic. Will you describe your topic from top to bottom, left to right, inside to outside, or in another way?

2 **Organize** the details from your Five Senses Chart in a word web.

See www.eduplace.com/kids/hme/ for graphic organizers.

Writing Similes

A **simile** uses the word <u>as</u> or <u>like</u> to compare two unlike things.

Similes	
	His cheeks were <u>as</u> red <u>as</u> strawberries.
	The rain sounded <u>like</u> a beating drum.

Try It Together

With your class, choose a classroom object. Think of other things that the object is like in some way. Work together to write a simile describing the classroom object.

▶ Write Your Similes

❶ Look at your Five Senses Chart and think about your topic.

❷ List objects that are like your topic in some way.

❸ Write two similes comparing your topic with two different objects.

Topic Sentence

A **topic sentence** tells the main idea of a paragraph in an interesting way.

Weak Topic Sentence	Strong Topic Sentence
This is what the storm last week was like.	The storm last week was really wild and a little scary too!

Try It Together

Work with your class to write some good topic sentences about your classroom or objects in it.

▶ Write Your Description

❶ **Write** two strong topic sentences for your description. Mark the one you like better.

❷ **Write** your description, using your word web. Include your topic sentence and similes.

How Good Is Your Description?

▶ **Read** your draft.

▶ **Copy** the sentences below that tell about your description.

Superstar

☐ I wrote about one thing, place, or event.

☐ My topic sentence is clear and interesting.

☐ I used lots of sensory words.

☐ I used exact adjectives and details to describe my topic.

☐ I used a simile to compare my topic to something else.

☐ My description has only a few mistakes.

Rising Star

☐ I described more than one thing, place, or event.

☐ I can make my topic sentence more interesting.

☐ I could use more sensory words.

☐ I need to add exact adjectives or details.

☐ I need to add a simile.

☐ My description has many mistakes.

See www.eduplace.com/kids/hme/
to interact with this rubric.

Unit 8: Description   **279**

▶ Revise Your Description

1 **Look** at the sentences from page 279 that you wrote about your description. What can you do to make your description better?

2 **Have a writing conference.**

When You're the Writer

- Write one question about a part of your description that you want help with.

- Share your description with a classmate. Ask your question.

When You're the Listener

- Tell two things you like about the description.

- Ask questions about parts that aren't clear.

- Look at the next page for more ideas.

3 **Revise** your description.

Think about your talk with your classmate. Make changes to your draft. The Revising Strategies on page 282 may help you.

- Change your topic sentence. Make it more interesting.

- Replace weak adjectives with strong ones.

📖 Use the Word Banks of sensory words in My First Thesaurus on page H45.

What to Say in a Writing Conference

If you are thinking . . .

You could say . . .

I don't have a clear picture of what you are describing.

What sensory words or details can you add to make this clearer?

There is no topic sentence.

Can you write a topic sentence to explain what you are describing?

This paper describes more than one topic.

What is the one topic you are describing?

Revising Strategies ⭐

Word Choice Adjectives help your readers see, hear, feel, taste, or smell what you are describing.

<u>large, red</u>
The fire engine raced down the street.
^

<u>screaming</u>   <u>spotted</u>
The siren was very loud. A dog sat in
^   ^

the back.

▶ Draw a line under each noun in your description. Can you add an adjective before each one to make your description clearer?

📖 Use My First Thesaurus on page H45 to find adjectives.

Sentence Fluency You may write two sentences that have the same naming part with different adjectives. Join the two sentences to make a longer one.

and yellow
The door was big. ~~The door was yellow.~~
^

▶ Look for places in your description where you can join two sentences.

▶ Proofread Your Description

❶ Proofread your draft. Use the Proofreading Checklist and the Proofreading Marks.

❷ Use a class dictionary to check spellings.

Proofreading Checklist

- ■ Each sentence begins with a capital letter.
- ■ Each sentence ends with the correct end mark.
- ■ Each paragraph is indented.
- ■ Each word is spelled correctly.

Proofreading Marks

∧	Add	≡ Capital letter
⌐	Delete	/ Small letter
¶	Indent for new paragraph	

Using the Proofreading Marks

Jade park has tall ~~tres.~~ trees.

One tree has a tire Swing.

❸ Review these rules before you proofread.

Grammar and Spelling Connections

Adjectives Add er to most adjectives to compare two things. Add est to most adjectives to compare more than two things.

The new jacket was warmer than the sweater.

The colorful snowsuit was the warmest of all.

Vowel Sounds The vowel sound in <u>cool</u> may be spelled oo.

food   pool   soon

📖 See the Spelling Guide on page H40.

▶ **Publish Your Description**

① Make a neat final copy of your description.

② Write an interesting title.

③ Look at Ideas for Sharing on the next page.

④ Publish or share your description in a way that works for your audience.

- Be sure you wrote all letters correctly and used good spacing. Check that you fixed every mistake.

- Begin the first, last, and each important word in your title with a capital letter.

▶ **Reflect**

Answer these questions about your description.

- What was easy about writing your description? What was hard?

- What do you like best about your description?

- Do you like your description better than other papers you have written? Why or why not?

Tech Tip If you wrote your description on a computer, fix all mistakes. Then print out a final copy.

Ideas for Sharing

Write It

- Write your description in a shape book.
- ★ Send your description in an e-mail to an aunt, uncle, cousin, or pen pal. · · · · · · · ·

> Always check for spelling mistakes before you send an e-mail.

Say It

- Recite all or part of your description. Use your body and your voice to help bring your description to life.
- Read it aloud in the Author's Chair.

Show It

- Draw pictures showing what you described.
- Add photos of your topic to your description.

Tech Tip
You can use different styles of letters to make your writing look more interesting.

Writing Prompts

Use these prompts for ideas or to practice for a test. Use sensory words and similes to make your description clear to your readers.

1 Write a description of a bakery or market that you have visited. Try to use words that describe what you taste, smell, feel, see, and hear.

2 Write a description of your favorite fruit. How does it look and smell before it is ready to eat? What does it taste like?

Writing Across the Curriculum

3 **FINE ART**

What is happening in this painting? What is the tiger doing? Use your senses as you write a description of the painting.

Henri J.F. Rousseau (Le Douanier) 1844-1910 National Gallery, London, UK/The Bridgeman Art Library

Tiger in a Tropical Storm (Surprised!) 1891 (oil on canvas)

See www.eduplace.com/kids/hme/ for more prompts.

Test Practice

Read this writing prompt.

Write a description of your <u>favorite fruit</u>. How does it <u>look</u> and <u>smell</u> before it is ready to eat? What does it <u>taste</u> like?

Follow these steps for writing to a prompt.

1 **Look** for clues that tell you what to write about. <u>Favorite fruit</u>, <u>look</u>, <u>smell</u>, and <u>taste</u> are clues.

2 **Look** for questions in the prompt. Answer the questions as you write.

3 **Think** about your topic. Make and fill in a chart like the one on this page.

Answering a Writing Prompt		
My Topic: my favorite fruit		
Looks?	Tastes?	Smells?

4 **Plan** your writing. Use a word web.

5 **Look** at page 279. What makes a Superstar?

6 **Write** your description.

Writing a Poem

The words in poems create pictures and make music. Some words sound like what they mean. Listen for sound words and rhyming words in these poems.

Wind Song

When the wind blows
the quiet things speak.
Some whisper, some clang,
Some creak.

Grasses swish.
Treetops sigh.
Flags slap
and snap at the sky.
Wires on poles
whistle and hum.
Ashcans roll.
Windows drum.

When the wind goes—
suddenly then,
the quiet things
are quiet again.

Lilian Moore

My Glider

My glider is graceful,
my glider is grand,
I launch it aloft
with a flick of my hand.
It smoothly ascends,
then it pauses and swoops,
it hovers in space
and turns intricate loops.

My glider is delicate,
nimble and rare,
it rises on gossamer
currents of air.
My glider is presently
useless to me—
my glider is stuck
in a very tall tree.

Jack Prelutsky

In these poems, listen for words that begin with the same sounds and for rhythm, or a pattern of beats.

Commas

Do commas have mommas
Who teach them to pause,
Who comfort and calm them,
And clean their sharp claws?
Who tell them short stories
Of uncommon commas
And send them to bed
In their comma pajamas?

Douglas Florian

Fishes' Evening Song

Flip flop,
Flip flap,
Slip slap,
Lip lap;
Water sounds,
Soothing sounds.
We fan our fins
As we lie
Resting here
Eye to eye.
Water falls
Drop by drop,
Plip plop,
Drip drop.
Plink plunk,
Splash splish;
Fish fins fan,
Fish tails swish,
Swush, swash, swish.
This we wish …
Water cold,
Water clear,
Water smooth,
Just to soothe
Sleepy fish.

Dahlov Ipcar

- What word describes the sound the treetops make in "Wind Song"? What words describe the sounds the flags make?

- What are the rhyming words in "My Glider"? Which lines rhyme?

- What beginning sound repeats in the first two lines of "Fishes' Evening Song"? What sounds repeat in lines 15, 16, and 19?

- How many beats do you hear in each line of "Commas"?

How to Write a Poem

1 **Choose** a topic. You can write a poem about almost anything—nature, an event, a favorite place, or a person.

HELP
?

Stuck for an Idea?

How about these?
- ▶ a color
- ▶ a kind of food
- ▶ a type of weather
- ▶ an animal
- ▶ a feeling

❷ Explore your topic by making an idea tree .

- Write your topic below the tree.

- Write verbs and adjectives about your topic on the trunk.

- Think of words that rhyme with your verbs and adjectives. Write those words on one of the big limbs.

- Think of words with the same beginning sounds as words on your tree. Write those words on the other big limb.

- Write sound words for your topic on the smaller branches.

soothe
flew   yum
plop
gold
smile
child
color
crunch
crisp
slurp   dreamy
sick
lips   drip
belt   sing
aloft

smooth
chew
cold
creamy
lick
melt
soft

Ice Cream

❸ Write your poem. Use words from your idea tree. End lines where you want your readers to pause.

> Which of these will you put in your poem?
> - sound words
> - rhyme
> - repeated beginning sounds
> - special rhythm

❹ Reread your poem. Do your words paint a clear picture of your topic? Does your poem have interesting sounds?

❺ Read your poem to a classmate. Think about your classmate's ideas.

❻ Revise your poem if you want to make changes.

❼ Proofread your poem. Use the Proofreading Checklist on page 283. Use a class dictionary to check spellings.

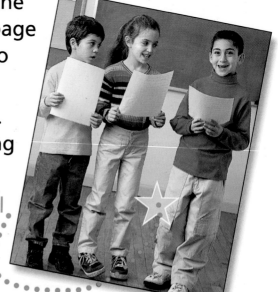

❽ Publish or share your poem. Make a neat final copy, using your best handwriting.

★ With a group, do a choral reading of your poem.

● Act out your poem as a classmate reads it aloud.

Writing a Shape Poem

A shape poem is a special kind of poem. Its shape helps readers see what the poem is about. Look at and listen to this shape poem.

Mushrooms Are Umbrellas

Mushrooms are umbrellas
for
ladybugs
and
their
fellas.

Arnold Spilka

How to Write a Shape Poem

1 **Choose** a topic that will be fun to write about and read about. You might choose a kite, a roller coaster, a seashell, an animal, or the moon.

2 **Think** about how you will use sound. Will you use rhyme or a special rhythm? Will you use sound words or repeat any beginning sounds?

3 **Write** your poem.

4 **Reread** your poem. Then read it to a classmate. Make any changes you want.

5 **Proofread** your poem.

6 **Publish** or share your poem. Draw your shape on a piece of paper. Write your poem inside it.

Giving a Talk

Giving a talk is a great way to share your work and your ideas. When you give a talk, show props such as pictures, objects, or charts to help explain what you mean.

Think and Discuss

- Why is everyone able to see the tiger picture?

- Is everyone able to see the guitar? Why or why not?

- Which part of the guitar is the girl talking about? How do you know?

- Where are the speakers looking? Why?

- What might they do differently if they were talking to the whole class?

Tips for Giving a Talk

▶ Begin speaking when your audience is ready to listen.
▶ Show pictures, objects, or charts.
▶ Be sure everyone can see you and your props.
▶ Look at your listeners and speak directly to them.
▶ Speak loudly enough for everyone to hear.
▶ Speak slowly and clearly.
▶ Use words that "fit" your listeners.

Apply It

Give a talk to your class or to a small group of classmates. Speak about a topic that you know and understand very well. Use the tips above to help you.

Stuck for a Topic?

How about these?
▶ a toy or model
▶ part of a collection
▶ how something works
▶ a favorite place

More Capitalization and Punctuation

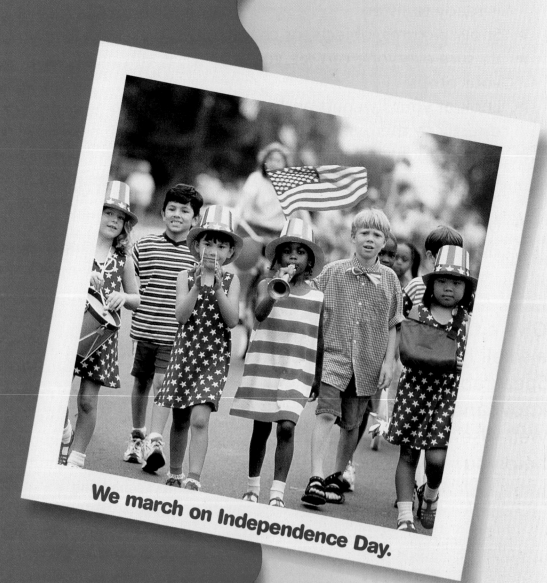

We march on Independence Day.

1 Days

How can you fix the answer to this riddle?

Riddle: On which day does it never rain?

Answer: sunday

There are seven days in a week. The names of the **days** of the week begin with **capital letters**.

Sunday	Monday	Tuesday	Wednesday
Thursday	Friday	Saturday	

Try It Out

Speak Up Read the sentences.
Tell which words need capital letters.

1. On tuesday I go food shopping.

2. Lian has a piano lesson on friday.

3. I have a meeting on wednesday.

4. On thursday we will plant a garden.

Write It Now write each sentence. Begin the name of each day correctly.

Example I need to call Tom on monday.

I need to call Tom on Monday.

Write the sentences. Use capital letters correctly.

Example John plays baseball on wednesday.

John plays baseball on Wednesday.

1. Clara's birthday is on saturday.

2. On monday I will clean the house.

3–6. Proofread this list of jobs. Find four mistakes with capital letters. Write the list correctly.

Example Take out the trash on tuesday.

Take out the trash on Tuesday.

Weekly Chores

Clean the hamster's cage on monday.
Set the table on Wednesday and friday.
Clean my room on saturday.
Rest on sunday!

Writing Wrap-Up
WRITING • THINKING • LISTENING • SPEAKING
INFORMING

Write a Weather Chart

List the days of the week. Write words and draw symbols to describe the weather each day. Discuss your chart with a classmate. Check for the correct use of capital letters.

    For Extra Practice, see page 330.

2 Holidays

Which holidays do the pictures make you think of? What have you learned about holidays?

Holidays are special days. New Year's Day and Thanksgiving Day are holidays. Each important word in the name of a **holiday** begins with a **capital letter**.

There are parades on **L**abor **D**ay.

People play jokes on **A**pril **F**ools' **D**ay.

Try It Out

Speak Up Read each sentence. Say the words that need capital letters.

1. Some people plant trees on arbor day.

2. Did you remember mother's day?

3. On columbus day, school is closed.

Write It Now write each sentence. Use capital letters correctly.

Example When is earth day?

When is Earth Day?

Write the sentences. Use capital letters correctly.

Example June 14 is flag day. June 14 is Flag Day.

1. January 1 is new year's day.

2. May 1 is may day.

3–6. Proofread a paragraph from Todd's journal. Find four mistakes with capital letters. Write the paragraph correctly.

Example I gave my dad a tie on father's day.

I gave my dad a tie on Father's Day.

Proofreading

I like holidays. We have a party at school on Valentine's Day. My family eats a big dinner on thanksgiving day. On memorial day, we honor those who died in wars.

Writing Wrap-Up WRITING • THINKING • LISTENING • SPEAKING

COMPARING & CONTRASTING

Write a Paragraph

Write about two holidays. Tell how they are alike and different. Read your paragraph to a classmate. Together, check for the correct use of capital letters in the names of holidays.

3 Months

Read the sentences. Which word names a month? How does the word begin?

Kiko wears her bathing suit. She sits in her pool. Now August feels cool.

—from A Year for Kiko, by Ferida Wolff

The names of the **months** begin with **capital letters**.

January	February	March	April
May	June	July	August
September	October	November	December

Try It Out

Speak Up Tell which words need capital letters.

1. In may we planted the seeds.

2. In june the plants began to grow.

3. Did the flowers bloom in july?

4. Some of them bloomed in august.

Write It Write each sentence correctly.

Example We planned the garden in march.

We planned the garden in March.

Write the sentences. Use capital letters correctly.

Example We gave a concert in may.

We gave a concert in May.

1. School started in august.

2. In november we had a field trip.

3–6. Proofread Abby's poem. Find four mistakes with capital letters. Write the poem correctly.

Example In october leaves fall from the trees.

In October leaves fall from the trees.

Proofreading

In january it may snow.

In march the wind may blow.

In june flowers grow.

In august there is grass to mow.

Writing Wrap-Up

WRITING • THINKING • LISTENING • SPEAKING

CREATING

Write a Poem

Write a poem about one or more months. Try to make some lines rhyme. Read your poem to classmates. Have them name each month and the capital letter with which it begins.

4 Titles for People

Read the sentence. What title is used before a person's last name? What other titles for people do you know?

The next morning Miss Nelson did not come to school.

—from Miss Nelson Is Missing! by Harry Allard

A **title** may be used before a person's name. A title begins with a capital letter and usually ends with a period. Read each name. Say the title. Which title does not end with a period?

Mrs. Mann   **Mr.** Chan   **Ms.** Willis

Miss Gomez   **Dr.** Rogers

Try It Out

Speak Up Read the names. Tell how to write each title correctly.

1. dr Lee

2. miss Santos

3. mrs Lane

4. ms Jackson

Write It Now write the titles and names correctly.

Example mr Smith Mr. Smith

Write the titles and names correctly.

Example mr. Li Mr. Li

1. miss Hill

3. Ms Vega

2. Mrs Bok

4. dr Hale

5–8. Proofread Hana's story. Find four mistakes with titles of people. Write the story correctly.

Example I bought my bike from mr Miller.
I bought my bike from Mr. Miller.

Proofreading

> I fell off my bike and broke my arm. My friend Mrs Lyon took me to the doctor. Dr. Davis put my arm in a cast. His nurse, ms. James, helped. Dr Davis called me miss Asato.

Writing Wrap-Up

WRITING • THINKING • LISTENING • SPEAKING

NARRATING

Write a Story

Write about someone visiting a doctor or dentist. Use people's names and titles in your story. Read your story aloud. Have a classmate name and spell each title.

5 Writing Book Titles

Make a list of your three favorite books. Compare your list with a classmate's list. Are any of the titles the same?

Swimmy
Iguana Beach
Dragon Gets By

In a **book title**, the first word, the last word, and each important word begin with a **capital letter**. The title is **underlined**. Short words like <u>a</u>, <u>an</u>, <u>and</u>, <u>the</u>, <u>in</u>, <u>for</u>, and <u>at</u> do not begin with a capital letter unless they are the first word in the title.

The book <u>The Cat in the Hat</u> is funny.

I read <u>A Birthday Basket for Tía</u> yesterday.

Try It Out

Speak Up Tell how to make each title correct.

1. abuela

2. frog and toad

3. nate the great

Write It Now write the book titles correctly.

Example the seashore book
<u>The Seashore Book</u>

Write the correct book title in each pair.

Example <u>My First American Friend</u> My First American Friend

<u>Danny and the dinosaur</u>

1. <u>My Pet Rabbit</u>

I'm Growing

2. <u>The great Ball Game</u>

<u>The Puddle Pail</u>

3–6. Proofread Antonio's letter. Find four mistakes with book titles. Copy the letter and write the titles correctly.

Example Mr. Putter and Tabby Take the train

<u>Mr. Putter and Tabby Take the Train</u>

Proofreading

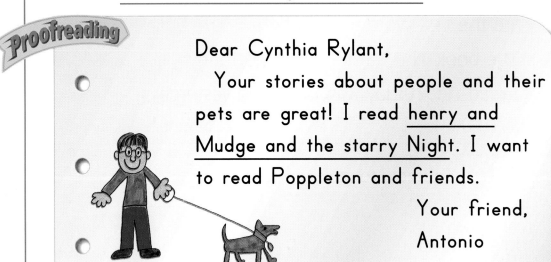

Dear Cynthia Rylant,

Your stories about people and their pets are great! I read <u>henry and Mudge and the starry Night</u>. I want to read Poppleton and friends.

Your friend,

Antonio

Writing Wrap-Up WRITING • THINKING • LISTENING • SPEAKING

EXPRESSING

Write a Letter

Write a letter to the author of a book you have read. Tell why you liked the book. Read your letter to a classmate. Work together to check that you wrote the book titles correctly.

  For Extra Practice, see page 334.

6 Ending Sentences

Look at these end marks. Say a sentence that ends with each mark.

A question ends with a **question mark**. An exclamation ends with an **exclamation point**. A command and a telling sentence end with a **period**.

Can we go fishing**?**   Clean your room first**.**

That is a great idea**!**   I will make lunch**.**

Try It Out

Speak Up Tell what kind of sentence each group of words is. Name the end mark that should be used.

1. Line up the turtles
2. My turtle is faster
3. Will it win the race
4. Hooray, my turtle won

Write It Write each sentence. Add the correct end mark.

Example I have a small turtle   I have a small turtle.

5. Your turtle is huge
6. What does it eat

Write each sentence. Add the correct end mark.

Example I am so excited   I am so excited!

1. We drive to the city

2. When will we get there

3–5. Proofread this tongue twister. Find three mistakes with end marks. Write the sentences correctly.

Example Sue sees some lights?   Sue sees some lights.

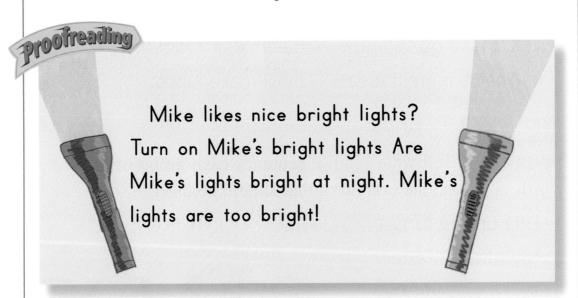

Mike likes nice bright lights?
Turn on Mike's bright lights Are
Mike's lights bright at night. Mike's
lights are too bright!

Writing Wrap-Up • WRITING • THINKING • LISTENING • SPEAKING

CREATING

Write Tongue Twisters

Write two kinds of sentences. Repeat letter sounds in the words you use. For example, Snakes slither slowly. Does Dan dance? Read your tongue twisters aloud. Have classmates say each one and tell what kind of sentence it is.

Writing Correct Sentences ⭐

Fixing Run-on Sentences A run-on sentence is really two sentences that should not be joined together. Turn a run-on sentence into two shorter sentences. Use **capital letters** and **end marks** correctly.

> **Wrong:** Dad looks up he sees stars.

> **Right:** Dad looks up. He sees stars.

Try It Out

Speak Up/Write It Read the run-on sentences. Turn each one into two shorter sentences. Say the two sentences. Then write them correctly.

Example   Sam looks at the sky the stars make pictures.
Sam looks at the sky. The stars make pictures.

1–2. Seven stars make a picture they look like a big spoon.

3–4. Three stars shine brightly they make a belt.

Revising Strategies continued

Apply It

1–9. Kate's e-mail letter has three run-on sentences. Copy the letter. Write each run-on sentence as two shorter sentences. Use end marks and capital letters correctly.

Example   The stars come out the stories begin.
The stars come out. The stories begin.

Revising

| Type Face ▼ | Size ▼ | B | *I* | u̲ | | Spell Check |

Dear Mom and Dad,

Gramps has a new telescope he got it last week. Gramps and I looked at the stars last night. He showed me some stars the stars made a picture of a bear. Gramps told me a story about the bear.

I looked at other stars. Some stars looked like a big ship it was sailing in the sky. Maybe I will write a story about that ship in the sky!

Love,

Kate

7 Commas in Dates

Neil Armstrong walked on the moon. When was he born?

Neil had been born in the living room of his grandparents' nearby farm on August 5, 1930.

—from *One Giant Leap: The Story of Neil Armstrong,*
by Don Brown

Every day has a date. A **date** tells the month, the number of the day, and the year. A **comma** (,) is used between the number of the day and the year.

Ali was born February 21, 1995.

She started school on September 2, 2000.

Try It Out

Speak Up Read each date. Tell where a comma belongs.

1. May 5 2000
2. June 30 2001
3. March 24 2002
4. April 7 2004

Born on
May 5, 2000

Write It Write the dates correctly.

Example November 23 1999 November 23, 1999

Write each sentence, using the correct date.

Example Tim was born on _____.

Tim was born on October 2, 1993.

1. I was born on _____.   **2.** Today is _____.

3–5. Proofread these events for Juanita's time line. Find three mistakes with commas in dates. Write each sentence and date correctly.

Example I lost my first tooth on May, 6 1998.

I lost my first tooth on May 6, 1998.

Proofreading

Time Line Events

I was born on June 22 1992.

I moved to Austin on August, 5 1996.

I started school on August 28, 1997.

My first day at camp was July 13 1998.

Writing Wrap-Up   WRITING • THINKING • LISTENING • SPEAKING

INFORMING

Write a Page for a Class Yearbook

Work with your class to make a chart of names and dates of class events this year. Then write a page about yourself. Include class events you enjoyed and their dates. Draw your picture. Have classmates check commas in dates.

8 Commas with Names of Places

One-Minute Warm-Up

List cities or towns and states that you know or would like to visit. Start with the name of the place where you live now. Can you find each place on a map?

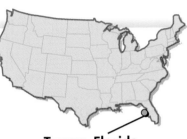

Tampa, Florida

Use a **comma** (**,**) between the name of a **city** or **town** and the name of a **state**.

> We watched fireworks in Miami, Florida.

> We went to a fair in Tyler, Texas.

Try It Out

Speak Up Read each place name. Tell where a comma belongs.

1. Lima Ohio

2. Portland Maine

3. Waco Texas

Write It Now write the names of the cities and states correctly.

Example Logan Utah Logan, Utah

Write each sentence. Put a comma in the correct place.

Example Nell is from Mesa Arizona. Nell is from Mesa, Arizona.

1. It gets cold in Nome Alaska.

2. Carlos moved to Salem Oregon.

3–5. Proofread this road sign. Find three mistakes with commas in place names. Write the sign correctly.

Example Boise Idaho 1711 miles

Boise, Idaho 1711 miles

Miles from Chicago, Illinois	
Detroit Michigan	279 miles
San, Antonio Texas	1209 miles
Miami Florida	1397 miles

Writing Wrap-Up

WRITING • THINKING • LISTENING • SPEAKING

DESCRIBING

Write a Paragraph

Write about where you live. Include the name of your town or city and state. Tell what you can see and do there. Read your paragraph to a classmate. Have the classmate check that you have used commas correctly with names of places.

9 Quotation Marks

Look at the picture. Say something funny that the porcupine might say if it could talk.

When you write, show what someone says by putting **quotation marks** (" ") at the beginning and end of the speaker's exact words.

Rosa said, "I know a joke."

Juan asked, "What is the joke about?"

Try It Out

Speak Up Read each person's exact words. Tell where quotation marks belong.

1. Rosa said, I like joke books.

2. Juan asked, Where can I get one?

Write It Now write the sentences correctly.

Example Juan said, That is a funny joke.

Juan said, "That is a funny joke."

Write each sentence. Put quotation marks around the speaker's exact words.

Example Joy said, Our class played a joke.

Joy said, "Our class played a joke."

1. Roy asked, What did you do?

2. Joy said, We switched seats.

3–5. Proofread these jokes. Find three sentences with missing quotation marks. Write the sentences. Put quotation marks where they belong.

Example Lee asked, What has four wheels and flies?

Lee asked, "What has four wheels and flies?"

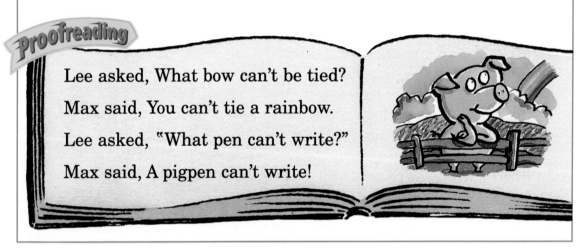

Proofreading

Lee asked, What bow can't be tied?

Max said, You can't tie a rainbow.

Lee asked, "What pen can't write?"

Max said, A pigpen can't write!

Writing Wrap-Up WRITING • THINKING • LISTENING • SPEAKING

NARRATING

Write a Conversation

Write what two people or animals say to each other. Name each speaker. Use quotation marks around each speaker's exact words. With a classmate, read aloud what each one says.

10 More About Quotation Marks

Read the exact words that Mother and Father said.

Mother and Father warned Baby Rattlesnake, "You must not use your rattle in such a way."

—from Baby Rattlesnake, told by Te Ata, adapted by Lynn Moroney

Follow these rules when you use quotation marks.

1. Put a **comma** after words such as <u>said</u> and <u>asked</u>.

2. Begin the first word inside the quotation marks with a **capital letter**.

3. Put the **end mark** inside the quotation marks.

> Hoshi said**,** "**M**y cat is lost**.**"

Try It Out

Speak Up Tell how to correct each sentence.

1. Leo said "mine can change colors!"

2. Ruby asked "What does it eat"

Write It Now write the sentences correctly.

Example Ruby asked "what can a lizard do"

Ruby asked, "What can a lizard do?"

1–6. Proofread this interview. Find six mistakes with commas, capital letters, and end marks in quotations. Two sentences are correct. The others have one mistake each. Write the sentences correctly.

Example: Paco asked "who owns that snake"

Paco asked, "Who owns that snake?"

Proofreading

Paco asked, "what kind of snake is that?"

The woman said, "It is called a boa"

Paco asked "How big is it?"

The woman said "It is ten feet long!"

Paco asked, "Does a boa close its eyes"

The woman said, "No, snakes have no eyelids."

Paco asked, "does a boa shed its skin?"

The woman said, "Yes, all snakes shed their skins."

Writing Wrap-Up   WRITING • THINKING • LISTENING • SPEAKING

EXPRESSING

Write an Interview

Ask three children this question. <u>What animal do you like best?</u> Use this sentence frame to record their exact words. <u>(Name)</u> said, "<u>(Answer)</u>." Read aloud your interview.

Enrichment

My Journal

- Make a journal to use next week. Use one page for each day. On the top, write the day of the week. Under that write the month, the number of the day, and the year.

- On each page, write about something you did that day. Draw a picture of it.

Sunday
May 17, 2001

I had a birthday party.

Sentence Worms

How old are you ?

I am seven years old .

- Write a question. Then write a sentence that answers the question.

- Cut out circles from colored paper. Write one word or end mark on each circle.

- Paste the circles in the correct order to make a question worm and an answer worm.

Challenge Mix up the circles for each sentence. Have a classmate make your two sentence worms.

Days and Holidays (pages 297, 299)

Write the sentences. Add a capital letter to each word that needs one.

1. My birthday is on wednesday.

2. We had a picnic on labor day.

Months (page 301)

Write the sentences. Add a capital letter to each word that needs one.

3. Mark went to camp in august.

4. In march Meg got a puppy.

Titles for People (page 303)

Write each title and name correctly.

5. mr. Nye

6. mrs Chan

Writing Book Titles (page 305)

Write the book title correctly.

7. letter to the lake

Ending Sentences (page 307)

Write each sentence. Add the correct end mark.

8. A dog barks at me

10. I am so afraid

9. Is the dog friendly

11. Don't run fast

Commas in Dates (page 311)

Write each date. Use commas correctly.

12. March 2 2001

13. May 15 2002

Commas with Names of Places (page 313)

Write the city and state. Use commas correctly.

14. Orlando Florida

15. San Jose California

Quotation Marks (pages 315 and 317)

Write the sentences. Add quotation marks,
an end mark, a comma, and a capital letter
to each sentence.

16. Mom asked how are you

17. Carla said i am fine

Mixed Review

18–25. Proofread this journal entry. Find eight mistakes with capital letters and punctuation marks. Then write the journal entry correctly.

Proofreading Checklist

✔ Do days, holidays, months, and people's titles begin with capital letters?

✔ Are book titles written correctly?

✔ Are commas used correctly in dates and names of places?

✔ Does a quotation have quotation marks, capital letters, a comma, and an end mark?

Example our vacation has been fun.

Our vacation has been fun.

Austin, texas

July 3, 2002

    I am having a great time in Texas. Today we visited the Alamo? I heard about all that happened there on march 6, 1836. mrs. Valero, our guide, asked, "did you know that Jim Bowie fought here?" I was the only one in our group who knew that.

    After our tour, we visited the gift shop. I bought a book called <u>heroes of the Alamo</u>. I will read it on our flight to Roswell New Mexico. We will spend independence Day there.

See www.eduplace.com/kids/hme/ for an online quiz.

Test Practice

Number a sheet of paper from 1 to 4. Read the paragraph and decide which type of mistake, if any, appears in each underlined sentence. Write the letter next to the correct answer. If the underlined sentence needs no change, write the letter next to "No mistake."

On Monday my sister got sick. Mom took Lisa to see dr.
(1)   (2)
Garza. He looked in her ears and throat. He said, Your throat is
                                          (3)
very red." Now Lisa has to stay home from school. Lisa can't
                                                   (4)
play with her friendes. She is sad. I hope she will be better soon.

---

1 A Spelling

   B Capitalization

   C Punctuation

   D No mistake

2 F Spelling

   G Capitalization

   H Punctuation

   J No mistake

3 A Spelling

   B Capitalization

   C Punctuation

   D No mistake

4 F Spelling

   G Capitalization

   H Punctuation

   J No mistake

Now write the numbers 5 to 8 on your paper. Read the paragraph and decide which type of mistake, if any, appears in each underlined sentence. Write the letter next to the correct answer. If the underlined sentence needs no change, write the letter next to "No mistake."

Have you ever been to San Antonio Texas? My Aunt
(5)
Mary lives there. We visited her last august. She took us to
(6)
the zoo. Do you know what I saw. I saw a baby tiger with its
(7)
mother. The baby tiger was named Stripes. Then we went to
(8)
the Alamo. We had a good time!

5 A Spelling

   B Capitalization

   C Punctuation

   D No mistake

6 F Spelling

   G Capitalization

   H Punctuation

   J No mistake

7 A Spelling

   B Capitalization

   C Punctuation

   D No mistake

8 F Spelling

   G Capitalization

   H Punctuation

   J No mistake

✓ Test Practice continued

Now write the numbers 9 and 10 on your paper. Read the paragraph and find the numbered, underlined parts. The underlined parts may be one of the following:

- Groups of words that are not sentences
- Run-on sentences
- Correctly written sentences that should be combined
- Correctly written sentences

Choose the best way to write each underlined part. Write the letter next to the correct answer. If the underlined part needs no change, write the letter next to "No mistake."

My school is near the park on Bell Street. My teacher is Mr. Ray he is a good teacher. On Friday he took our class to the park. He asked us to draw pictures of nature. Sara saw a black bird. John saw a black bird. Sara drew a picture of the bird.

9 A My teacher is Mr. Ray. He is a good teacher.

B My teacher. Is Mr. Ray. he is a good teacher.

C My teacher is Mr. Ray. Is a good teacher.

D No mistake

10 F Sara and John. Saw a black bird.

G Sara and John saw a black bird.

H Sara and John saw. A black bird.

J No mistake

Unit 1: The Sentence

Naming Part and Action Part (pages 29–32)

Write each sentence. Circle the naming part. Draw a line under the action part.

1. Dad and I went to the zoo.

2. The huge lion roared.

3. The tall giraffe ate leaves.

4. The seal swam around.

Which Kind of Sentence? (pages 37–46)

Write each sentence correctly. Tell if it is a telling sentence, a question, a command, or an exclamation.

5. the gift is for Emma

6. what is it

7. open it

8. i love this hat

Unit 3: Nouns and Pronouns

Nouns (pages 93–96)

Write the sentences. Draw a line under each noun.

9. Is the girl cold?

10. The grass is wet.

One and More Than One (pages 97–98, 101–104)

Write each noun to name more than one.

11. box   **12.** cat   **13.** man

Pronouns (pages 107–108)

Write each sentence, using a pronoun in place of the underlined word or words. Use <u>he</u>, <u>she</u>, <u>it</u>, or <u>they</u>.

14. <u>Donna</u> got a bike.

15. <u>The bike</u> is red.

Nouns Ending with ’s and s’ (pages 113–116)

Write each sentence, using the correct noun.

16. My bike is much older than (Jims’, Jim’s) bike.

17. The two (dogs’, dog’s) leashes are the same color.

Unit 5: Verbs

Verbs That Tell About Now and About the Past

(pages 165–166, 169–170)

Write each sentence, using the correct verb.

18. Meg and Pat (dance, dances) well.

19. Meg (give, gives) dance lessons.

20. Last week Meg (plants, planted) her garden.

Special Verbs (pages 173–182)

Write each sentence, using the correct verb.

21. Paco's best friend (went, gone) to camp with him.

22. The camp (is, are) on a lake.

23. The boys and girls have (saw, seen) a rainbow.

24. The campers (was, were) tired after the hike.

Contractions (pages 183–184)

Write the contractions for these words.

25. do not

26. does not

Unit 7: Adjectives

How Something Looks, Tastes, Smells, Sounds, and Feels (pages 239–244)

Write sentences by matching each word group in Box **A** to an adjective in Box **B**.

A	B
27. The color of his hat is	loud.
28. The music sounds	cold.
29. The water feels	red.
30. The campfire smells	big.
31. The soup tastes	smoky.
32. The tent is	salty.

Special Adjectives (pages 247–250)

Write each sentence, using the correct word in ( ).

33. Are ants (smaller, smallest) than worms?

34. Does (a, an) octopus live in the ocean?

Unit 9: More Capitalization and Punctuation

Days, Holidays, and Months (pages 297–302)

Write the sentence correctly.

35. The first monday in september is labor day.

Titles for People and Books (pages 303–306)

Write the titles correctly.

36. ms kent

37. dear zoo

Commas: Dates, Place Names (pages 311–314)

Write the date and place name correctly.

38. August 17 2001

39. Miami Florida

Quotation Marks (pages 315–318)

Write the sentence correctly. Add quotation marks, a comma, an end mark, and a capital letter.

40. Sam asked where do you swim

(pages 297–298)

1 Days

- Begin the names of days of the week with capital letters.

Remember

●▲ Find the word in each sentence that needs a capital letter. Then write the sentences correctly.

Example On tuesday we gave a puppet show.

On Tuesday we gave a puppet show.

1. The spelling test is on wednesday.

2. Our class is having a party on friday.

3. On thursday our class has gym.

■ Answer each question with a sentence that names a different day of the week.

Example When is your favorite TV show on?

My favorite TV show is on Monday.

4. What is your favorite day?

5. When don't you go to school?

6. When do you go to school?

(pages 299–300)

2 Holidays

- Begin each important word in the name of a holiday with a capital letter.

●▲ Look at each pair of sentences. Write the sentence in which the holiday is written correctly.

Example We have a vacation on columbus Day.
We have a vacation on Columbus Day.
We have a vacation on Columbus Day.

1. February 14 is Valentine's Day.

February 14 is valentine's day.

2. We ate turkey on Thanksgiving day.

We ate turkey on Thanksgiving Day.

3. Dad made dinner on mother's Day.

Dad made dinner on Mother's Day.

■ Find the words that need capital letters. Then write each sentence correctly.

Example When is flag day? When is Flag Day?

4. Friends visit on new year's day.

5. Did you forget father's day?

6. What day is labor day?

7. Why do we celebrate earth day?

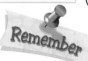

(pages 301–302)

3 Months

• Begin the names of months with capital letters.

Remember

●▲ Find the word in each sentence that needs a capital letter. Write the sentences correctly.

Example Jason read four books in november.

Jason read four books in November.

1. It snowed in january.

2. In april it rained a lot.

3. It was hot in august.

4. In october he saw pumpkins.

■ 5–8. Find the word in each sentence that needs a capital letter. Then write the story sentences correctly.

Example They sold their house in july.

They sold their house in July.

They moved to Florida in september. In february Rosa got a new puppy. In march her mother started a new job. They planted a big garden in may.

(pages 303–304)

4 Titles for People

- Begin a title before a person's name with a capital letter.
- Put a period after Mrs., Mr., Ms., and Dr.
- The title Miss does not have a period.

●▲ Write the titles and special nouns correctly.

Example dr pang Dr. Pang

1. miss lee
2. mr vega
3. ms kemp
4. mrs shaw

■ **5–8.** Copy this story. Write the four titles and last names correctly.

Example First, mr klein wiggled his ears.

First, Mr. Klein wiggled his ears.

The neighbors tried to make my baby sister smile. If mrs ito tickled Sally, would she smile? Sally didn't smile. Funny dr santos flapped his arms like a bird. Sally didn't smile. ms stone jumped up and down. Sally didn't smile. Then miss shaw made a funny face. Sally didn't smile. Finally, they went home. Sally smiled!

Extra Practice

5 Writing Book Titles

(pages 305–306)

- Begin the first word, last word, and each important word in a book title with a capital letter.
- Draw a line under the title.

Remember

●▲ Write the book titles correctly.

Example brothers and sisters

Brothers and Sisters

1. dragon gets by

2. ben and me

3. too many tamales

■ Write each sentence and its book title correctly.

Example I read ira sleeps over

I read Ira Sleeps Over.

4. Ron read mrs. brown went to town.

5. Jill read ramona the pest.

334   Extra Practice

(pages 307–308)

6 Ending Sentences

- A telling sentence and a command end with a period. (.)
- A question ends with a question mark. (?)
- An exclamation ends with an exclamation point. (!)

Remember

●▲ Write the correct sentence in each pair.

Example I am hungry. I am hungry.
When can I eat.

1. Do you like ice cream.
   This tastes great!

2. Do you want more?
   Wipe your mouth?

■ Write the sentences. Add
the correct end marks.

Example It is my birthday
It is my birthday.

3. Will I get gifts

4. Look in the kitchen

5. What a surprise

6. The kitten is for me

(pages 311–312)

7 Commas in Dates

- A date tells the month, the number of the day, and the year.
- Use a comma (,) between the number of the day and the year.

Remember

●▲ Write each date. Use commas correctly.

Example July 4 1776

July 4, 1776

1. May 16 2001

2. June 12 1990

3. August 9 2004

■ Write the sentences and finish each one with the correct date. Use commas correctly.

Example Joe was born on _____.

Joe was born on September 25, 1996.

4. Today is _____.

5. School began on _____.

6. Next New Year's Day is _____.

7. My birthday is _____.

(pages 313–314)

⑧ **Commas with Names of Places**
- Use a comma (,) between the name of a city or town and the name of a state.

Remember

●▲ Write each city and state. Put commas in the correct places.

Example Niagara Falls New York

Niagara Falls, New York

1. Chico California

2. Denton Texas

■ Write the sentences.
Put commas in the correct places.

Example My aunt lives in Stowe Vermont.

My aunt lives in Stowe, Vermont.

3. An airport is in Orlando Florida.

4. My family drove through Oxford Ohio.

5. Brownsville Texas is near the Mexican border.

(pages 315–316)

⑨ Quotation Marks

- Put quotation marks (" ") at the beginning and end of the speaker's exact words.

Remember

●▲ Write each sentence. Draw a line under the speaker's exact words.

Example Marta said, "We wrote our names backward."

Marta said, "We wrote our names backward."

1. Marta said, "Today was Backward Day."

2. Dad asked, "What is that?"

3. Marta said, "We put our clothes on backward."

4. Dad asked, "Did you walk backward too?"

■ Write each sentence correctly. Add quotation marks.

Example Jim asked, Do you have a pet?

Jim asked, "Do you have a pet?"

5. Sam said, I have a dog.

6. Jim asked, What is its name?

7. Sam said, His name is Rex.

8. Jim said, I like dogs.

(pages 317–318)

10 More About Quotation Marks

- Put a comma after words like <u>said</u> and <u>asked</u>.
- Begin the first word inside the <u>quotation marks</u> with a capital letter.
- Put the end mark inside the quotation marks.

Remember

●▲ Write the correct sentence in each pair. Be sure to copy commas, capital letters, and end marks correctly.

Example Mom asked, "What animal is this?"
Mom asked, "What animal is this"
Mom asked, "What animal is this?"

1. Nan said, "it looks like a snake."
   Nan said, "It looks like a snake."

2. Mom said "It is a fish called an eel"
   Mom said, "It is a fish called an eel."

3. Nan asked, "How does an eel swim?"
   Nan asked, "How does an eel swim"?

■ Write each sentence correctly. Add a comma, end mark, and capital letter.

Example Max asked "what is that"
Max asked, "What is that?"

4. Dad said "it is a starfish"

5. Mom said "it has five arms"

Writing to Express an Opinion

A shark is an amazing fish.

Listening to an Opinion Essay

In "My Life in the Country," the writer gives his opinion, or tells how he feels, about living in the country. What is the writer's opinion? What are some of the reasons the writer gives to explain the way he feels?

My Life in the Country

by Tomie dePaola

I live in the country and I love it. When I was young, I grew up in a small city that had a busy "downtown" with stores and restaurants, ice cream parlors, and movie theaters. One summer, my whole family went on a real go-away vacation to Vermont. We went through little towns, past red barns, farm houses, and big meadows. It was the very first time I had seen the real COUNTRY, and I fell in love with it. I remember saying to myself, "When I grow up, I'd like to live in the country, just like Vermont." New Hampshire, where I live now, is right next door to Vermont and just as much "country."

Why do I like living in the country? First of all, I like the peace and quiet. I like to hear the birds singing in the early morning. I like to see the fresh dew on the meadow first thing in the morning during the summer, and the frost in the fall, and the snow in the winter and early spring. I like seeing the sun hit the top of Mount Sunapee at dawn. I like seeing all the stars at night because there are no city lights to block them out.

Another reason I like living in the country is that I have the right atmosphere to do my writing, drawing, and painting. There are not many distractions, no noisy traffic, no crowds of people. My ideas have a nice place to grow just like the wildflowers that I see alongside the roads when I take an early morning walk.

In the winter, I like looking out and seeing the deer eating the leftover apples on the apple trees. And I have a whole flock of crows that live in the meadow all year. The way they walk and "talk" to each other keeps me smiling all day long.

I travel often and get to visit cities all over the world, but I'm always happy to get home to my house in the country. Nothing is nicer than to wake up early and have a cup of tea while looking out the window at the meadow. I watch my crows. I think about the day's work ahead. I am very happy.

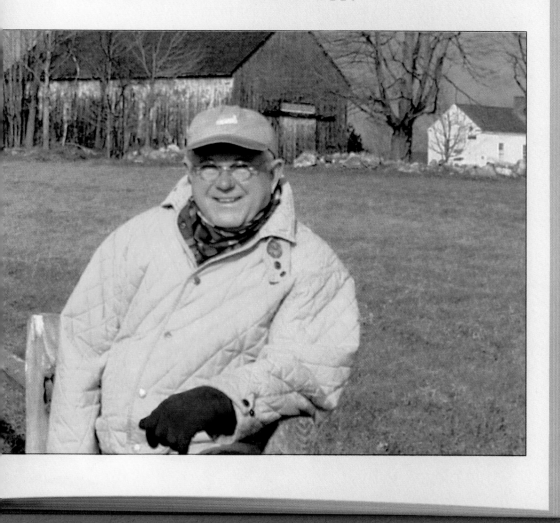

Reading As a Writer

Think About the Opinion Essay

- What is the writer's opinion of living in the country?

- What are two of the reasons that the writer gives to explain his opinion?

Think About Writer's Craft

- Why do you think the writer capitalized all of the letters in the word <u>COUNTRY</u>?

Think About the Pictures

- On pages 341–343, how do the pictures show you that the writer likes living in the country?

Responding

Write an answer to this question.

- **Personal Response** How do you feel about the country after reading this piece? Why?

What Makes a Great Opinion Essay?

In an **opinion essay**, you tell why you like or dislike something. When you write an opinion essay, remember to do these things.

▶ Begin by writing your opinion. Tell what you like or don't like.

▶ Write at least two good reasons for your opinion.

▶ Add examples to explain each of your reasons.

▶ Use words that let your readers know how strong your feelings are.

▶ End your essay by using different words to write your opinion again.

GRAMMAR CHECK

When you write a sentence, use the form of the verb that goes with the naming part.

WORKING DRAFT

Read Phillip's draft that tells why he likes school. Then read what W.R. said about it.

Phillip A. Jackson

| Type Face ▼ | Size ▼ | **B** | *I* | <u>u</u> | | Spelling |

Can you give another example telling how your teachers are nice?

I think school is terrific. I like school because the teachers are nice. They let us walk to lunch by ourselves and play games outside.

Another thing I like about school is reading books. I read the Berenstain Bears books and the Horrible Harry books. I can check out books to read at the school library.

Good! You wrote a new paragraph for your second reason.

School is gr-r-reat!

The words in this sentence really let me know how strong your feelings are.

Reading As a Writer

- What are the two reasons Phillip likes school?
- What could Phillip do to make his ending better?

Read Phillip's final copy and what W.R. said about it.

Good! You began by writing your opinion clearly.

School Is Gr-r-reat!
by Phillip A. Jackson

Beginning your sentence with these words helps me know that this is your first reason.

I think school is terrific. First of all, I like school because the teachers are nice. They help us with our work. They also let us walk to lunch by ourselves and play games outside.

Another thing I like about school is reading books. I read books about the Berenstain Bears and Horrible Harry. I can check out books to read at the school library.

I really like school because of the nice teachers and the books I read. I think school is gr-r-reat!

Now your last paragraph really sums it all up!

Reading As a Writer

- What example did Phillip add to help explain that the teachers are nice?
- What did Phillip add to make his last paragraph better?

Write an Opinion Essay

▶ **Choose Your Topic**

1 List three things that you like a lot or that you don't like at all.

2 Tell a classmate what you like or dislike about each topic idea. Then answer these questions.

- Which topic did you explain best?

- Which topic do you have the strongest feelings about?

3 Copy and complete these sentences. Name your audience and topic.

_____ will read or hear my opinion essay.

I will write about _____.

HELP
? **Stuck for an Idea?**

How about these?
▶ a subject in school
▶ foods
▶ sports or games
▶ holidays

See page 360 for more ideas.

▶ **Explore Your Topic**

① **Think** about your topic. List reasons why you feel the way you do about your topic.

② **Look** at the chart Phillip used to list the reasons he likes school.

Opinion Chart
My opinion: I like school.

Reason 1: nice teachers	Reason 2: reading books

③ **Make** a chart like the one Phillip made. Write your opinion and at least two reasons why you like or do not like your topic.

④ **Show** your chart to a classmate. Explain your reasons clearly. Do the reasons make sense to your classmate?

⑤ **Think** about what your classmate said. Make changes to your chart.

See www.eduplace.com/kids/hme/ for graphic organizers.

Focus Skill

Explaining with Examples

When you write an opinion, use good examples to explain each of your reasons.

Try It Together

Why do you like recess? With your class, write some strong examples that explain each reason.

▶ Plan Your Opinion Essay

❶ **Look** at the examples Phillip added to his Opinion Chart to explain his reasons.

Opinion Chart	
My opinion: I like school.	
Reason 1: nice teachers	Reason 2: reading books
Example 1: They let us walk to lunch by ourselves.	Example 1: I read the Berenstain Bears and Horrible Harry books.
Example 2: They let us play games outside.	Example 2: I check books out at the library.

❷ **Add** boxes to your Opinion Chart and write two examples to explain each reason.

 See www.eduplace.com/kids/hme/ for graphic organizers.

Focus Skill

Openings and Closings

Your opinion essay needs a strong opening and closing. Your **opening** is how you start the essay. Your **closing** is how you end the essay.

Weak Opening	Strong Opening
I like Dallas.	Dallas is an exciting city.

Weak Closing	Strong Closing
So that's what I think about Dallas.	Dallas is a city with many interesting sights to see.

Try It Together

With your class, choose a fun activity you have done together. Work together to write a strong opening and closing for an essay telling why you liked the activity.

▶ **Write Your Opening and Closing**

❶ **Write** a strong opening for your opinion essay.

❷ **Write** a strong closing for your opinion essay. Tell your opinion again, using different words.

Focus Skill

Writing with Voice

In your opinion essay, use powerful words to show how strong your feelings are.

Weak Voice	Strong Voice
I like living in the country.	I live in the country, and I **love** it.
School is fun.	I think school is **terrific**.

Try It Together

Work with your class to rewrite the sentence below. Use words that will show your strong feelings.

I think spelling contests are fun.

amusing
exciting
thrilling
interesting
pleasant

▶ **Write Your Opinion Essay**

❶ **Begin** your opinion essay by copying your opening on another sheet of paper.

❷ **Write** a paragraph to explain each reason in your Opinion Chart. Include examples to explain each reason.

❸ **End** your essay by copying your closing.

Remember:
Powerful words add
voice to your essay.

How Good Is Your Opinion Essay?

▶ **Read** your draft.

▶ **Copy** the sentences below that describe your essay.

Superstar

☐ My opening is interesting and tells my opinion clearly.

☐ I included at least two good reasons and some examples for my opinion.

☐ I used words that show my strong feelings.

☐ My closing retells my opinion.

☐ My writing has only a few mistakes.

Rising Star

☐ My opening could tell my opinion more clearly.

☐ I can add more reasons and examples for my opinion.

☐ I can use stronger words to show my feelings.

☐ My closing could retell my opinion better.

☐ My writing has many mistakes.

See www.eduplace.com/kids/hme/ to interact with this rubric.

Unit 10: Opinion Essay **353**

▶ **Revise Your Opinion Essay**

① **Look** at the sentences from page 353 that you wrote about your opinion essay. What can you do to make your essay better?

- Write a new opening. Is it stronger than your first opening?
- Add examples to explain your reasons.

② **Have a writing conference.**

When You're the Writer

- Write one question that you have about your opinion essay.

- Share your essay with a classmate. Ask your question.

When You're the Listener

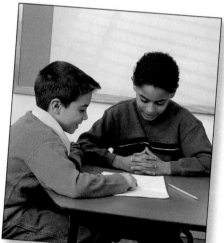

- Tell two things you like about the essay.

- Ask your classmate for more examples if you don't understand a reason.

- Look at the next page for more ideas.

③ **Revise** your opinion essay. Think about what you and your classmate talked about. Make changes to your draft to make it better. The Revising Strategies on page 356 may help you.

What to Say in a Writing Conference

If you are thinking . . .   **You could say . . .**

The opening does not state the opinion clearly.

What other words could you use to tell your opinion?

The reasons don't make sense.

How can you state your reasons in a different way?

There are no examples to explain the reasons.

What examples can you add that tell about each reason?

Revising Strategies

Word Choice Write exact nouns, adjectives, and verbs to make your writing clearer.

> love   bake   Ana
> I ~~like~~ to ~~cook~~ with Grandma.
>   bake tasty apple pies
> We ~~make good things.~~

▶ Find two places in your essay to add exact words.

📖 Use My First Thesaurus on page H45 to find exact words.

Sentence Fluency You can make short sentences with the same naming part into one long sentence. Use commas to do so.

> Rex is the best dog! ~~Rex is cute.~~
> Rex is cute, friendly, and playful.
> ~~Rex is friendly. Rex is playful.~~

▶ Try to find one place in your essay where you can join short sentences into one long one, using commas.

▶ Proofread Your Opinion Essay

❶ Proofread your draft. Use the Proofreading Checklist and the Proofreading Marks.

❷ Use a class dictionary to check spellings.

Proofreading Checklist

- ☐ Each sentence begins with a capital letter.
- ☐ Each sentence ends with the correct end mark.
- ☐ Each sentence has a naming part and an action part.
- ☐ Each word is spelled correctly.

Proofreading Marks

∧ Add	≡ Capital letter
๑ Delete	/ Small letter
¶ Indent for new paragraph	

Using the Proofreading Marks

Soccer is great! it is so
              ≡

exciting when I scores a goal.

❸ Review these rules before you proofread.

Grammar and Spelling Connections

Verbs and Naming Parts When you write a sentence, use the form of the verb that goes with the naming part.

Damon and Ed read books.

Chen reads the newspaper.

Final Consonant Sounds A final consonant sound may be spelled with two letters that are the same.

off   fell   class

📖 See the Spelling Guide on page H40.

▶ Publish Your Opinion Essay

❶ Make a neat final copy of your opinion essay.

❷ Write an interesting title.

❸ Look at Ideas for Sharing on the next page.

❹ Publish or share your essay in a way that works for your audience.

- Be sure you wrote all letters correctly and used good spacing. Check that you fixed every mistake.
- Begin the first, last, and each important word in your title with a capital letter.

▶ Reflect

Answer these questions about your opinion essay.

- What do you like most about your opinion essay? Why?

- What did you learn while writing your opinion essay?

- Do you like this paper better than other papers you have written? Why or why not?

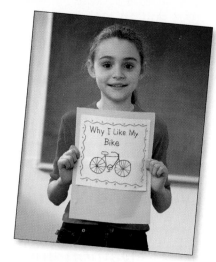

Why I Like My Bike

Tech Tip
If you wrote your opinion essay on a computer, fix all mistakes. Then print out a final copy.

Ideas for Sharing

Write It

- Post your essay on your school's Internet site.
- Share your essay in a class newspaper or a school newsletter.

Say It

- Read your essay to members of your family. Discuss whether or not they agree.
- Send a recording of your essay to someone who might like to listen to it.

Show It

- ★ Display your essay on a poster. Add photos or drawings.
- Cut pictures from magazines. Make a collage to go with your essay.

Make sure you choose photos or drawings that really help to show your opinion.

Writing Prompts

Use these prompts for ideas or to practice for a test. Remember to include reasons and examples to explain your opinion.

1 What is your favorite animal? Write an opinion essay explaining why you like that animal.

2 Write an opinion essay about a chore you do not like to do.

Writing Across the Curriculum

3 **SOCIAL STUDIES**

Write an opinion essay about a place you visited. Tell what you liked and disliked about it.

4 **SCIENCE**

How do you feel about spiders? Write an opinion essay explaining how you feel about them.

5 **HEALTH**

What is your favorite dessert? Write an opinion essay explaining why you like it.

6 **LITERATURE**

Write an opinion essay about a character from a book. Tell what you like and dislike about the character.

 See www.eduplace.com/kids/hme/ for more prompts.

✓ Test Practice

In an opinion essay, you can write what you like about a topic.

Read this writing prompt.

What is your <u>favorite animal</u>? Write an <u>opinion essay</u> explaining why you <u>like</u> that animal.

Follow these steps for writing to a prompt.

❶ Look for clues that tell you what to write about. The words <u>favorite animal</u>, <u>opinion essay</u>, and <u>like</u> are clues.

❷ Look for questions that you should answer. What question is in the prompt above?

❸ Plan your writing. Use an Opinion Chart like the one on page 350.

❹ Look at page 353. What makes a Superstar?

❺ Write your opinion essay.

Writing to Persuade

When you write to persuade, you try to get your audience to do something. Read this **persuasive essay** that Maurice wrote and what W.R. said about it.

> ## Why Everyone Should Help Clean Our Park
>
> Everyone likes going to a park because it is so much fun there. Kids love to go to play, and grown-ups like to go for picnics and to be with family and friends. Nobody goes to our neighborhood park, though, because it is dirty. Everyone in our neighborhood should help clean up our park.
>
> A dirty park is not a beautiful place. Our park looks terrible because paper and litter are everywhere. People do not enjoy being there because it is such a mess.
>
> A dirty park is unsafe. People don't want to go to a park where they have to worry about stepping on broken glass. Also, if we clean our park, parents will not have to worry about their children getting hurt.

Your audience will know exactly what you want them to do. You stated your **goal** clearly.

These are strong **reasons** with good **facts** and **examples**.

The next time you visit our park, remember how important it is to make it clean. Do your part to help make our park a clean, beautiful, and safe place to be.

> You **reminded** your audience of what they should do. You **summed up** your goal and your reasons.

Reading As a Writer

- What is Maurice's **goal**?

- What two **reasons** does Maurice give to persuade people to clean up the park? What **facts** and **examples** does he write for each one?

- In which sentence does Maurice **remind** his **audience** of his goal?

How to Write to Persuade

1 **List** three goals that you feel strongly about.

2 **Talk** with a classmate. Answer these questions about each goal.

- Do I feel strongly about this goal?

- Who will read or hear my paper?

- Can my audience really do what I want them to do?

- Can I think of two strong reasons to help persuade my audience?

3 **Copy** and **complete** these sentences. Name your goal and your audience.

I will write about _____.

_____ will read or hear my essay.

HELP

Stuck for a Goal?

Here are some ideas to think about.

- ▶ My family should _____.
- ▶ The students in our school should _____.
- ▶ Our whole class should _____.

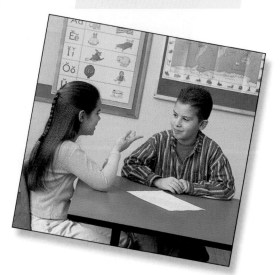

4 **Explore** your goal. Why do you think it is important? Why should your audience do what you suggest? Strong reasons will help you persuade your audience. Look at the web Maurice made to explore his goal.

Goal

Everyone in our neighborhood should help clean up our park.

Reason

It's not a beautiful place.

Reason

It's not safe.

Now make a web like the one Maurice did. Write your goal in the large circle. Think of two strong reasons for your goal. Write one reason in each of the smaller circles.

5 **Think** about your reasons. Facts or examples for each reason will make your goal even stronger. Look at the facts and examples Maurice added to his web.

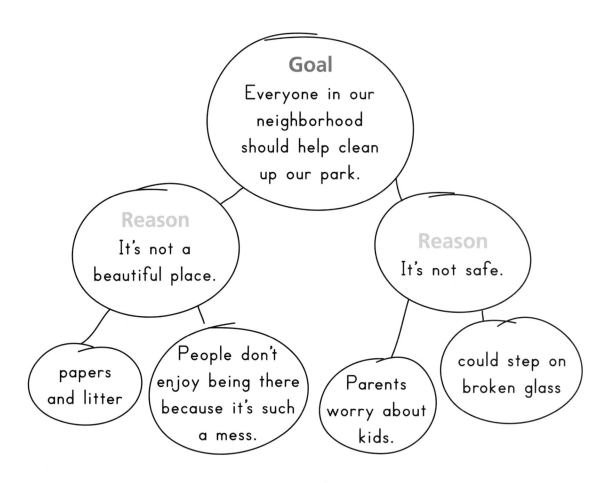

Add to your web. Draw circles connected to each reason. Think of facts or examples for each one. Write one fact or example inside each circle.

6 **Draft** your persuasive essay.

- Write a paragraph that states your goal in a clear and interesting way.

- Write one paragraph for each reason. Include your facts or examples.

- Write a paragraph that sums up your reasons. Remind your audience of what you want them to do.

7 **Look** at the checklist. What can you do to make your persuasive essay better?

Revising Checklist

- ☐ I tell my goal in a clear and interesting way.
- ☐ I give two reasons for my goal.
- ☐ I include facts or examples for each reason.
- ☐ I sum up my reasons to remind my audience of what I want them to do.

8 **Have** a writing conference. Take notes to remember your classmate's ideas.

What to Say in a Writing Conference

If you are thinking . . .   You could say . . .

I don't understand the goal.

What do you want your audience to do?

Why should anyone do that?

Can you tell me some reasons for your goal?

That reason makes no sense.

Could you explain that reason? Tell me some facts or examples about it.

9 **Revise** your essay. Think about what you and your classmate talked about. Make changes to your essay.

10 **Proofread** your essay. Use the Proofreading Checklist on page 357. Use a class dictionary to check your spelling.

⑪ Publish or share your essay in a way that works for your goal and your audience. Make a neat final copy, using your best handwriting. Write an interesting title for your essay.

★ Present your essay to your audience as a speech. See Giving a Talk on pages 294–295 for tips.

● Publish your essay in a class newspaper or on your school's Web site.

Tech Tip
If you wrote your essay on a computer, fix every mistake. Then print out a final copy.

Comparing Media

Thinking About Media

Newspapers, radio, and television are all **media**. You can get news and information from different kinds of media. Each one gives news in a different way and can change how you feel and think about the news.

We are bringing you a live report from Palm Bay. There is a rescue team working hard to save a beached whale. You can see that the tide is coming in, and this beautiful whale is already being moved toward deep water.

Whale Beached in Palm Bay
At dawn today, a fisherman reported a beached whale. A rescue team hopes to move the whale to safety some time today.

There's a report of a beached whale in Palm Bay. The tide is coming in, and a rescue team is hoping to have the whale back in deep water by late afternoon.

Think and Discuss

Look at the pictures above and think about the media. How are they the same? How are they different?

Thinking About Ads

Have you ever seen an ad for a toy and thought you just had to have it? Ads, or advertisements, are used to get people to buy or do something. You might see ads in magazines, on huge signs called billboards, or on television.

Ads use words and pictures that are attractive and eye-catching. Some ads also use sound. You might hear a tune you like that makes you remember the product in the ad.

Apply It

What do the magazine ad and billboard ad try to get people to do? Do you think the ads work? Why or why not?

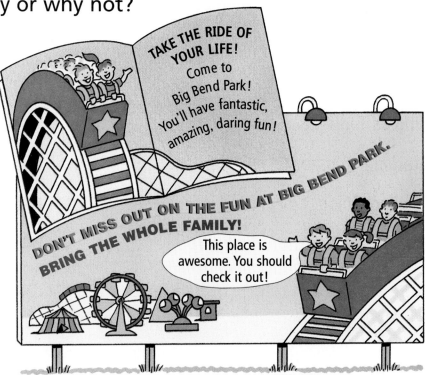

Tools
and
Tips

ABC Order

The letters of the alphabet are in ABC order.

A B C D E F G H I J K L M

N O P Q R S T U V W X Y Z

Words can also be put in ABC order. Are these words in ABC order?

ant   **b**ig   **c**at

The words are in ABC order. Use the first letter of each word to put words in ABC order.

Try It Out

Speak Up Say these words in ABC order.

dog   **i**nk   **g**ame   **e**at

Write It 1–4. Now write the words in ABC order.

1–8. Copy the alphabet. Write the missing letters.

A _ C D E _ G H _ J K L _

N O P _ R S _ U V _ X _ Z

Write the words in each box in ABC order.

9.

> **p**et
>
> **o**pen
>
> **n**ine

10.

> card
>
> with
>
> my
>
> sky

11.

> bear
>
> map
>
> hot

12.

> send
>
> glass
>
> hen
>
> zoo

More ABC Order

You know that you look at the first letters of words to put them in ABC order.

Sometimes two words begin with the same letter. When this happens, look at the second letter in each word. Why does <u>ba</u>t come before <u>bo</u>y?

bat   **bo**y   **bu**g

Try It Out

Speak Up Say these words in ABC order.

sell	**sw**im	**sa**t	**sn**ow

Write It 1–4. Now write the words in ABC order.

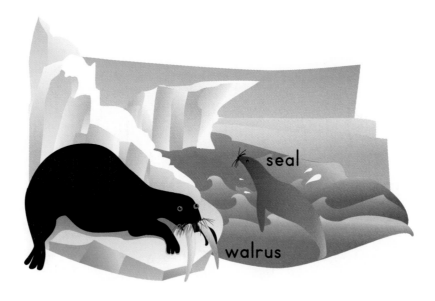

seal

walrus

Write the words in each box in ABC order. Look at the second letter of each word.

1.
> **bl**ue
>
> **ba**ll
>
> **bu**s

2.
> tan
>
> trip
>
> top

3.
> stand
>
> sting
>
> small

4.
> fox
>
> fly
>
> find

5.
> run
>
> ride
>
> rock

6.
> like
>
> let
>
> lunch

The Dictionary

A **dictionary** is a book about words. The words a dictionary tells about are in **dark print**. They are called **entry words**. Entry words are in ABC order.

Entry Words

S

S

seed
A **seed** is part of a plant.

ship
A **ship** is a big boat.

Try It Out

Speak Up Answer each question with a word from the Word Box.

and	dig
girl	now

1. Which word is between <u>cap</u> and <u>fish</u>?

2. Which word is between <u>get</u> and <u>grew</u>?

3. Which word is between <u>mine</u> and <u>open</u>?

4. Which word is between <u>air</u> and <u>boy</u>?

Write It 1–4. Now write the words.

Write the word from the Word Box that comes between each pair of entry words.

| box | need | arm | eat |

1. baby ____ cap

2. day ____ fall

| school | sun | some | swim |

3. see ____ stamp

4. sad ____ seat

| gym | give | grow | gave |

5. get ____ glass

6. good ____ gull

| money | noise | quack | rock |

7. pear ____ ride

8. like ____ nice

| crow | carry | clam | cent |

9. chop ____ corn

10. copy ____ cub

Research and Study Strategies

Finding Word Meanings

A dictionary tells the meanings of words. Look at the dictionary entry for <u>mirror</u>. What is the meaning of <u>mirror</u>?

Entry Word   **Meaning**

M m

mirror

A **mirror** is piece of glass you can see yourself in.

Research and Study Strategies

Try It Out

Speak Up Tell the meaning of <u>fog</u>.

fog

Fog is a cloud that is near the ground.

Write It Now write <u>fog</u> and its meaning.

Write each word and its meaning. Use the dictionary meanings shown on this page.

1. storm   **2.** stripe   **3.** subway

storm

A **storm** is a strong wind with rain or snow.

stripe

A **stripe** is a wide line.

subway

A **subway** is a train that travels underground through tunnels.

Research and Study Strategies

More Than One Meaning

One word can have more than one meaning. The dictionary explains each meaning. Each meaning is numbered.

How many dictionary meanings does the word <u>wing</u> have?

wing

1. A **wing** is a part of a bird, a bat, and some insects.

2. A **wing** is a part of a plane. It sticks out like the wing of a bird.

Research and Study Strategies

Try It Out

Speak Up Tell which meaning of <u>wing</u> fits each sentence.

1. The bird hurt its <u>wing</u>.
2. I sat by a <u>wing</u> on the plane.
3. I can see the silver <u>wings</u> of the plane.
4. Bees have two pairs of <u>wings</u>.

Write It 1–4. Write each sentence. Then write **1** or **2** to show which meaning of <u>wing</u> fits the sentence.

Write each sentence. Then write **1** or **2** to show which meaning of <u>chest</u> fits each sentence.

chest

1. The **chest** is a part of the body. It is below the shoulders and above the stomach.

2. A **chest** is a strong box.

1. Mother put the pictures in the chest.

2. Father is sunburned on his chest.

3. Ed has a pain in his chest.

Write each sentence. Then write **1** or **2** to show which meaning of <u>spot</u> fits each sentence.

spot

1. A **spot** is a small mark that is not the same color as the area around it.

2. A **spot** is a place.

4. Peter dropped the penny in this spot.

5. Lin got a black spot on her red dress.

6. The dog hid its bone in this spot.

Title Page and Table of Contents

The **title page** is the first important page in a book. It lists the book's title, author, and publisher.

The **table of contents** of a book shows the chapters, or parts, of the book. It shows the page where each chapter begins.

Try It Out

Speak Up   Find the title page on the first page of this book. Say the title of this book.

Write It   Look at the table of contents of the book below. It has three chapters. Write the answers to each question.

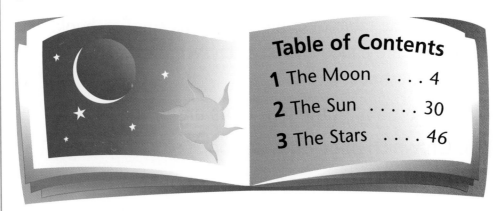

Table of Contents
1 The Moon 4
2 The Sun 30
3 The Stars 46

1. What is the title of Chapter 2?

2. On which page does Chapter 1 begin?

3. "The Stars" is the title of which chapter?

Write the answers to the questions below. Use this table of contents.

Table of Contents

1. How many chapters are shown?

2. What is the title of Chapter 1?

3. What is the title of Chapter 2?

4. On which page does Chapter 3 begin?

Look at the table of contents for this English book. The chapters are called **units**. Then write the answers to these questions.

5. How many numbered units are in the book?

6. On which page does Lesson 1 of Unit 5 begin?

7. In Unit 9, what lesson is on page 301?

Using the Library

You can find books to read at your school or town library. A library is set up in a special way so that you can find the books you want quickly and easily.

Fiction One part of your library has fiction books. These are stories that are made up by an author. These books are put on the shelves in ABC order by the last names of the authors.

Nonfiction Another part of your library has nonfiction books. These books tell facts about real people, animals, places, and events. Nonfiction books are grouped by subjects such as science or history. They are given special numbers to help you find them.

Reference Reference books are found in one section. An atlas (a book of maps), a dictionary, and an encyclopedia are reference books. These may also be stored on CD-ROMs that can be used on a computer.

Book-Finding Tools You can find books in the library by using a card catalog. A **card catalog** is a set of drawers with cards that list books in ABC order by the author's last name, the book title, or the subject.

Most libraries today have an **electronic catalog** stored on a computer. You can search for a book if you know either the book's title or author. You can also type in the name of the subject and find books about that subject.

Using an Encyclopedia

An encyclopedia is a set of books that gives information about many topics such as famous people, places, things, and events. The facts are found in pieces of writing called **articles**.

Encyclopedia articles are put in ABC order in books called **volumes**. Most volumes are labeled with one letter. Everything written about in that volume will begin with that letter. Some volumes may have more than one letter. There are also CD-ROM and online versions of encyclopedias.

Using Visuals: Graphs

A **graph** is a drawing that shows information in picture form. It can help you understand and compare numbers of people or things.

A **bar graph** shows numbers, using colored boxes or bars. Look at this graph one class made showing their favorite fruits.

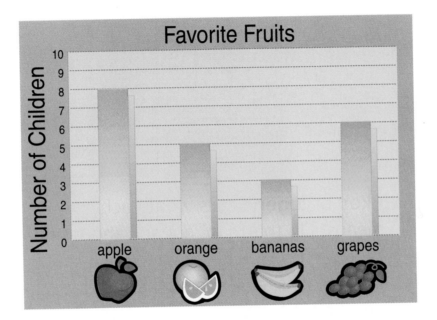

The **title** tells what the graph is about. The **labels** give more information. The label at the side shows the number of children. The labels under the bars or boxes show the different choices of favorite fruits.

To read this graph, look at the number beside the line that the top of each bar reaches.

Using Visuals: Maps

A **map** is a simple drawing showing all or part of a place. You may have seen a road map or world map with the outlines of countries. The map below shows most of North America.

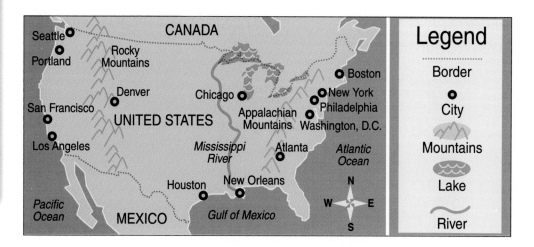

A **map key** or **legend** tells what each symbol on the map means. On this map, a black and orange dot stands for a city. The blue areas and lines show water—lakes, oceans, and rivers. The red dotted lines show where the United States meets Canada and Mexico. Small triangles show mountains.

The **compass rose** beside the legend shows directions on a map—north (**N**), south (**S**), east (**E**), and west (**W**).

Open-Response Questions

On some tests, you must read a paragraph or story and then write one or two complete sentences to answer a question about it. Remember these tips to help you write a good answer.

Tips for Answering an Open-Response Question

1. Read the question carefully. Try to use part of the question in your answer.
2. Think about what you read. What words, sentences, or ideas might answer the question?
3. Answer only the question that is asked.
4. Write your answer neatly in complete sentences.

Read the book summary below. Write sentences telling why the little house was unhappy.

A little house lived way out in the quiet country. It liked to watch the days and seasons come and go.

Then one day builders came. They built roads, houses, stores, and tall buildings. It became noisy and crowded all around the little house. The little house was now living in a city!

The city was too bright and noisy. Nobody noticed the little house anymore. It was squeezed between bigger buildings. The little house was unhappy.

Think and Discuss Read these two answers to the question. Which one is a better answer? Why?

Answer 1

The little house liked living in the country. Then they built things all around the house I would like to live in the country.

Answer 2

The little house was unhappy because it wanted to live in the country and not in a crowded city. The little house was sad because nobody noticed it.

In the **first answer**, the writer does not tell why the little house was unhappy but instead tells what happens. The writer also gives information that the question does not ask for. The answer ends with a run-on sentence.

In the **second answer**, the writer uses words from the question. The writer uses information from the book summary to explain why the little house is unhappy. Only information that is asked for is given. The writer uses capital letters and end marks correctly to write two complete sentences.

Computer Talk and Technology Terms

CD-ROM a round disk on which numbers, words, and images can be stored and then read, heard, or viewed on a computer

cursor a marker on a computer screen, which may or may not flash, that shows where information can be entered

data the basic information that you get from a computer or that can be put into and understood by a computer

disk a magnetic object on which computer programs and data can be stored

document a piece of writing that you create on a computer

floppy disk a small plastic disk that is used to store computer data

font any one of many styles of letters that a computer can make

Times
Courier
Helvetica

hard copy information from a computer that is printed on paper

hard drive a large disk inside the computer that holds more data and works faster than a floppy disk

hardware the parts of a computer including the keyboard, monitor, memory, and printer

Internet a large computer network that connects computers around the world

key any button on a keyboard with a letter, number, word, or symbol

keyboard the part of the computer made up of a set of keys

memory the part of the computer in which information is stored

menu a list of choices within a computer program that are usually shown on the screen

modem a machine that allows computers to communicate with other computers over telephone lines

monitor the part of the computer that shows the information on a screen

mouse the part of a computer that you move with your hand to move the cursor around the screen and make choices

printer the part of the computer that puts information on paper

software programs that let people do things such as type, play games, and draw pictures on computers

Using a Computer

A computer is an amazing tool! Read these pages to find out about some of the things you can do with it.

Games for Learning

Do you know that there are many games on CD-ROM and floppy disk that can help you learn? Some Web sites on the Internet also have games that you can open and play.

There are computer games that can help you become a better writer, review letters and sounds, practice math skills and problem solving, and learn about people and places.

Drawing and Writing

Have you ever written a story or a poem that you wanted to illustrate? You can use a computer to draw pictures and diagrams to go with your writing.

Some computer software gives you space to write and to draw a picture. Other programs let you insert a drawing, a diagram, or a chart anywhere within your writing. You can also choose a picture from a list to put into your document.

The Big Game

By José Perez

The Internet

The **Internet** is a network of computers from all over the world. It connects people, classrooms, companies, libraries, museums, and other interesting places. Here are some of the many things you can do on the Internet.

- Use a search tool to help you find Internet sites on topics that interest you. Type in a key word or phrase about your topic.

- Connect to the World Wide Web. You can find lots of information in places called Web sites. Each Web site has its own address.

Tech Tip
Visit us on the Internet at www.eduplace.com.

- Send e-mail to your friends or family. See Using E-mail on the next page for more tips.

- Create your own Web page. Design the page, write the text, and choose links to other sites.

Using E-mail

E-mail is a great way to write and receive messages quickly from people all over the world. Read the message below.

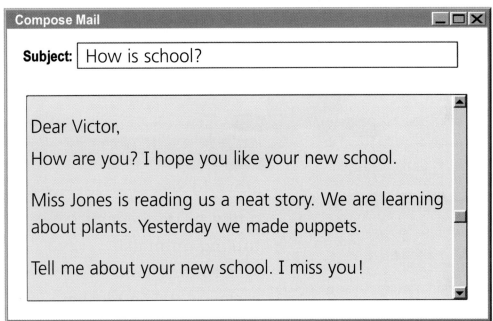

Compose Mail

Subject: How is school?

Dear Victor,

How are you? I hope you like your new school.

Miss Jones is reading us a neat story. We are learning about plants. Yesterday we made puppets.

Tell me about your new school. I miss you!

E-mail Tips

- Type a title in the subject line.
- Keep your paragraphs short.
- Skip a line instead of indenting when you begin a new paragraph. Your message will be easier to read.
- Do not use special type such as italics or underlining. It may not show up on the other person's screen.
- Follow the rules of good writing.
- Proofread your message. Check for missing capital letters and end marks. Fix all spelling mistakes.

Computers and the Writing Process

Try writing your next story, letter, report, or poem on a computer. Read these pages to learn how.

Choose New Folder from the menu of your writing software. Give your folder a name.

PREWRITING

List your topic or story ideas in a new document.

> **Word Processor- STORY IDEAS**
> File Edit View Insert Format Help
>
> Story Ideas
>
> a day at the beach
> talking animals
> kids finding gold
> a class with no teacher

Discuss your ideas with a classmate. Add new ideas to your list. Then choose your topic.

Explore your topic. Add details you would like to include in your writing. Save your document in your folder.

Create a story map or other graphic organizer that you can use to help you plan your writing. See page H31 for help with using graphic organizers.

DRAFTING

Print out your prewriting documents. Use them as you write your working draft.

Open a new document and name it <u>Working Draft</u>.

Set your computer for double spacing. This will give you room between lines to write your changes after you print your document.

Type your thoughts as you think of them. Do not worry about completing your sentences or grouping ideas together. You can make changes later.

Save your document early and often!

REVISING

Have a conference

with a classmate. Print your working draft. Read your draft aloud and discuss any questions or problems. Take notes to remember your classmate's ideas.

Remember to save your working draft and place it in your folder.

Open your working draft and choose Save As from the menu. This makes a second copy of your document. Name this document Second Draft.

Make changes to your writing. Add, cut, or move words and sentences. Use commands from the menu or special keys on the keyboard to help you do this.

Copy	copies text you select
Cut	removes text you select
Delete key	removes text letter by letter
Paste	puts copied or cut text into a document
Return key	moves the cursor to the next line
Save	saves your changes
Shift key	lets you type a capital letter
Spelling	starts the spelling tool

Using Technology

Proofread your sentences by turning them into a list.

- Place the cursor after each end mark and press <u>Return</u>.
- Fix sentences that are either too long or too short, do not begin with capital letters, or do not end correctly.
- After you proofread, just delete the extra returns.

A spelling tool can help you proofread your writing. However, it cannot find and fix some mistakes.

- It cannot tell the difference between words that sound the same but are spelled differently such as <u>tale</u> and <u>tail</u>.
- It cannot find a mistake that is the correct spelling of another word. For example, you type <u>hid</u> but want <u>hide</u>.
- It does not know if two words should be one word such as <u>mail</u> <u>box</u>.

Think of a spelling tool as a proofreading partner!

Choose <u>Save As</u> from the menu. Name this new document Final Copy.

Using Technology

Using Technology

Choose letter styles and type sizes that you like and that can be easily read.

Add artwork to your final copy. Use page breaks so that a small part or paragraph is on each page. Then use computer clip art or a drawing program. You can also print the pages and draw or paste pictures on them.

Print your final copy. Then place the document in your writing folder on the computer.

Now that's a JOB WELL DONE!

Graphic Organizers

You may have many ideas for a story or report. Which one will you write about? What will you write about your topic? How can you organize your ideas before you write? These graphic organizers can help!

Idea Wheel

Use an **idea wheel** to help you think of ideas to write about. In each section, write or draw ideas of people, animals, places, or things that you could write about.

Describing Wheel

Use a **describing wheel** to write details about someone, something, or someplace. Write your topic in the middle of the wheel. List describing words that tell about your topic in the spaces between the spokes.

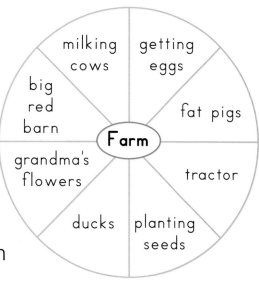

See www.eduplace.com/kids/hme/ for graphic organizers.

Tools and Tips

Word Web

Use a **word web** to organize your details about a topic. Write your topic in a circle in the middle of the page. Then write details about your topic around it. Circle each detail. Draw a line from the circled detail to the topic in the middle.

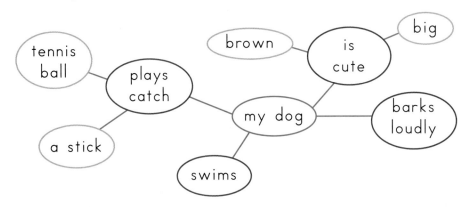

Tree Chart

Use a **tree chart** to show a topic and its details. Write the topic or main idea on the trunk. Write the details on the branches. Add as many branches as you need.

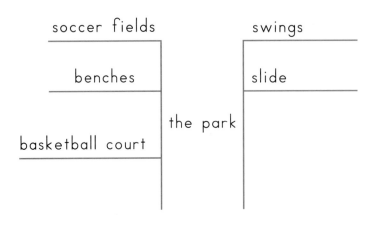

Story Map

Use a **story map** to help you plan your story. In the Beginning box, name the main characters, write where and when your story will take place, and tell what the problem is. In the Middle box, write what will happen in your story and how the characters are working to solve the problem. In the End box, write how the problem is solved.

Beginning
cat, dog, animal friends in the woods summer Cat falls into deep hole.

Middle
The dog asks friends how to get the cat out. They try to help.

End
They use a ladder to get the cat out of the hole. The friends have a party.

Five W's Chart

Use a **five W's chart** to list important details about an event. Your readers will want to know who, what, when, where, and why.

Five W's Chart
What happened?   a puppet show
Who was there?   Ms. Rowe's class
Why did it happen?   to tell some fairy tales
When did it happen? Tuesday at 10 o'clock
Where did it happen?   in room 8

Spider Map

Use a spider map to list ideas and details about a topic. Write the topic in the center circle. Write main ideas on lines that go out from the center circle. Then write details that support each main idea.

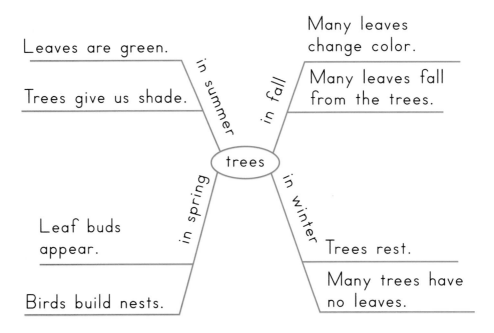

Sequence Chart

Use a **Sequence Chart** to help you put in order the steps for instructions or the events for a story.

Sequence Chart	
Topic	Planting Seeds
First	Dig holes in the dirt.
Next	Put the seeds in each hole.
Last	Cover the seeds with dirt and water them.

Grammar, Usage, and Mechanics Terms

action part
the part of a sentence that tells what the naming part did or does

Andre **wrote a story**.
We **walk to school**.

adjective
a word that describes how someone or something looks, tastes, smells, sounds, or feels

The **tall** man walks **two** dogs in the **big** park.
The **red** roses smell **sweet** and feel **smooth**.

adverb
a word that describes a verb by telling how, when, or where

Ed ate **quickly**.
I rode my bike **today**.
My dog went **out**.

apostrophe
(') a mark added to nouns to show ownership
This mark is also used in place of missing letters in a contraction.

Lynn's cat purred softly.
The twins' room is messy.
The baby isn't asleep yet.

capital letter
an uppercase letter that is used to begin a sentence, a special noun, the first word in a quotation, and the first, last, and each important word in a book title

Most winters are warm in **F**lorida.
Scott asked, "**W**here does **A**nna live?"
Carmen read <u>**T**he **B**ig **B**alloon **R**ace</u>.

comma
(,) a mark used in dates, between a city or town and state, in quotations, and after words in a series

Zach was born on March 23**,** 1993.
He lives in Austin**,** Texas.
Inez asked**,** "Do you see a cat**,** a dog**,** and a bird?"

command
a sentence that tells someone to do something
It begins with a capital letter and ends with a period.

Clean your room.

complete sentence
a sentence that has a naming part and an action part

The children|swim in the pool.

contraction
a short way of writing two words
An apostrophe shows where letters were left out.

The word **doesn't** is the contraction for <u>does</u> <u>not</u>.

exclamation and exclamation point
a sentence that shows strong feeling; it begins with a capital letter and ends with an exclamation point (**!**).

I won! Please hurry!

helping verbs <u>has</u> and <u>have</u>
verbs that help other verbs show actions that happened in the past

Abby **has** given me a gift.
We **have** seen the beavers at Long Pond.

naming part
the part of a sentence that tells who or what did or does something

Dad fished in the stream. **The book** falls off the bed.

noun
a word that names a person, an animal, a place, or a thing

The **children** rode on the **bus**.
Four **frogs** jumped out of the **pond**.

period
(.) a mark used to end a telling sentence or a command

Dinosaurs are no longer living. Open the window.

pronoun
a word that takes the place of one or more nouns

Pedro and Callie play soccer. **They** are on the same team.
Kate studied stars. **She** learned about hot gases.

question and question mark
a sentence that asks something; it begins with a capital letter and ends with a question mark (**?**).

How old are you?

quotation marks
(**" "**) marks used to begin and end a person's exact words

Shawn said, **"**Let's play tag.**"**
Suki asked, **"**What is for lunch?**"**

run-on sentence
two sentences that have been incorrectly joined together as one sentence
It should be written as two shorter sentences, each with a naming part and an action part.

Ali lost her book a friend found it. (wrong)
Ali lost her book. A friend found it. (right)

sentence
a group of words that tells or asks what someone or something did or does
It begins with a capital letter and ends with a period, a question mark, or an exclamation point.

Nan read a book. Can you draw? I won a prize!

special adjectives <u>a</u> and <u>an</u>
They come before nouns that name one.

An insect walked on **a** leaf.

special noun

a noun that names a special person, animal, place, or thing
A special noun begins with a capital letter.

Corey e-mails his friend.
I patted my kitten, **Midnight**.
We went to the zoo in **San Diego**.
I saw the **Statue of Liberty**.

telling sentence

a sentence that tells something
It begins with a capital letter and ends with a period.

Mike likes to swim.
Jasmine learned to ski.

title

a word or abbreviation that can be used before a
person's name
A title is also used to name a book.

Miss Ramon is sick today.
She wants to call **Dr.** Harding.
My favorite book is **James and the Giant Peach**.

verb

a word that shows action or being now or in the past

Pablo **hits** the baseball.
Ling **kicked** the soccer ball.
Tony **is** the winner of today's race.
Mandy **was** the winner last week.

Words Often Misspelled

You use many of the words on this page in your writing. Check this list if you cannot think of the spelling for a word you need. The words are in ABC order.

A

again
always
am
and
are

B

because
before

C

cannot
coming
could

D

down

F

family
for
friend
from

G

getting
girl
goes
going

H

have
here
how

I

I'm
it
it's

K

knew
know

L

letter
little

N

name
new
now

O

on
other
our
outside

P

pretty

R

really
right

S

said
school
some
something
started

T

that's
their
there
through
time
tried

V

very

W

want
was
went
were
where
would
write

Y

you
your

Spelling Guidelines

1. A **short vowel** sound may be spelled **a**, **e**, **i**, **o**, or **u**.

   h**a**t p**e**t p**i**n t**o**p f**u**n b**a**g t**e**n m**i**x f**o**x m**u**d

2. The long **a** sound may be spelled **ai**, **ay**, or **a**-consonant-**e**.

   m**ai**l   tr**ai**n   w**ay**   pl**ay**   m**a**d**e**   **a**t**e**

3. The long **e** sound may be spelled **e**, **ee**, or **ea**. At the end of a two-syllable word, it may be spelled **y**.

   b**e** w**e** k**ee**p gr**ee**n r**ea**d cl**ea**n man**y** happ**y**

4. The long **i** sound may be spelled **i**, **y**, **igh**, or **i**-consonant-**e**.

   f**i**nd kind fl**y** sk**y** h**igh** l**igh**t n**i**n**e** f**i**v**e**

5. The long **o** sound may be spelled **o**, **oa**, **ow**, or **o**-consonant-**e**.

   g**o** c**o**ld b**oa**t c**oa**t sl**ow** sh**ow** th**o**s**e** h**o**m**e**

6. The long **u** sound may be spelled **u**-consonant-**e**.

   c**u**t**e**   **u**s**e**   m**u**l**e**   h**u**g**e**

7. The vowel sounds in **moon** and **book** may be spelled **oo**.

   f**oo**d   r**oo**m   l**oo**k   g**oo**d

8. The vowel sound in **town** and **out** may be spelled **ow** or **ou**.

   c**ow** n**ow** br**ow**n m**ou**se h**ou**se f**ou**nd

9. The vowel sound in **fog**, **paw**, and **call** may be spelled **o**, **aw**, or **a** before **ll**.

| dog | log | saw | draw | ball | small |

10. The vowel + **r** sounds may be spelled **ar**, **or**, or **ore**.

| arm | car | for | born | more | store |

11. The sound at the end of **flower** is a vowel + **r** sound. This sound is spelled **er**.

| sister | after | father | over | better | water |

12. Two consonant letters whose sounds are blended together are called a **consonant cluster**.
A **consonant cluster** may be spelled **br**, **gl**, **st**, **tr**, **cl**, and **sw** at the beginning of words or **st** and **xt** at the end of words.

| brave glad step trip club swim nest lost next |

13. Some words end with consonant sounds spelled **nd**, **ng**, and **nk**. You hear the sounds of **n** and **d** in words that end with **nd**. You may not hear the **n** sound in words that end with **ng** or **nk**.

| end | hand | king | bring | think | thank |

14. The sound that begins **when** may be spelled **wh**.
The sound that begins **then** and ends **teeth** may be spelled **th**.

| which wheel what while than them with both |

15. The sound that begins **sheep** and ends **wish** may be spelled **sh**. The sound that begins **chase** and ends **much** may be spelled **ch**.

| **sh**ip | wa**sh** | **ch**op | ea**ch** |

16. The consonant sound at the end of **stick**, **speak** and **lake** may be spelled **ck** or **k**.

| ki**ck** | ro**ck** | as**k** | for**k** | ba**k**e | hi**k**e |

17. A final consonant sound may be spelled with the **same two letters**.

| wi**ll** | o**ff** | a**dd** | e**gg** | dre**ss** |

18. Some words have the vowel-consonant-**e** pattern. The **final e** in these words is **dropped** before **ed** or **ing** is added.

| us**e** | hop**e** | rid**e** | lik**e** | nam**e** | clos**e** |
| using | hoping | riding | liked | named | closed |

19. Some words end with a short vowel sound followed by one consonant. The **final consonant** in these words is usually **doubled** before **ed** or **ing** is added.

| hu**g** | ge**t** | ru**n** | sto**p** | ba**t** | gra**b** |
| hu**gg**ing | ge**tt**ing | ru**nn**ing | sto**pp**ed | ba**tt**ed | gra**bb**ed |

20. To name more than one, add **s** to most words. Add **es** to words that end with **s**, **x**, **sh**, or **ch**.

| day**s** | thing**s** | dress**es** | box**es** | dish**es** | inch**es** |

21. **Homophones** are words that **sound alike** but do not have the same spelling or meaning.

plain	road	tail	hole
plane	rode	tale	whole

22. A **compound word** is a word that is made up of two shorter words.

bedtime	anyone	maybe	bathtub	upon	into

23. A **contraction** is a short way of writing two words. An apostrophe (') takes the place of the letter or letters that are left out.

I'll	we've	you're	don't	doesn't	isn't	can't

How to Use This Thesaurus

A thesaurus can help you find just the right words to use when you write. Imagine you wrote this sentence.

My birthday gift came in a **big** box.

You decide that big doesn't tell how big the box really was. You need a more exact word. What can you do? You can look in this thesaurus to find other words for big.

1. First, find the word big. Remember that the entry words in a thesaurus are in ABC order. Since big begins with b, you would look in the section with B words.

B

big having great size
The elephant is so **big**!

huge
large

2. Next, read the meaning of the word big.

3. Then read the sample sentence. You can see that huge and large are words you could use in place of big.

4. Last, rewrite your sentence, using a more exact word.
Here is an example.

Your first sentence: My birthday gift came in a **big** box.

Your new sentence: My birthday gift came in a **huge** box.

My First Thesaurus

A
---

afraid filled with fear

The bird is **afraid** of the cat.

    frightened

    scared

---

argue to have a quarrel

They **argue** about the treat.

    disagree

    squabble

WORD BANK: Action Words

Use strong action words like these when you write.

climb	march	skip
crawl	ride	slide
dance	roll	walk

B
---

big having great size

That elephant is so **big**!

    huge

    large

---

brave facing danger or pain without fear

You are very **brave**, Mr. Bear.

    bold

    courageous

    fearless

C

choose to pick out, after thinking about what is best

I will **choose** a dress to wear.

decide on
select

cold having no warmth

The wind is **cold** today.

chilly
freezing
frosty

cry to shed tears because of sadness or pain

Please don't **cry**, Little Bear.
sob
wail
weep

D

do to carry out an act

I will **do** my work now.
complete
finish

E

eat to take food into the body

They **eat** the corn.
consume
dine on
gobble up
munch

WORD BANK: Words That Tell How Things Feel

Use words like these to tell how things feel.

cold	hard	soft
crumbly	rough	sticky
dry	smooth	warm

find to get something by looking for it

Will she **find** the kitten?

> discover
> locate
> spot

fun a good time

Playing soccer is **fun**!

> enjoyable
> entertaining

go to pass from one place to another

I will **go** as fast as I can.

> advance
> move on
> progress

good having fine qualities

That is a **good** sand castle!

> terrific
> wonderful

H

happy feeling pleasure

I was **happy** to see Uncle Ken.
    delighted
    glad

help to do what is needed or useful

I **help** Mrs. Wills.
 aid
 assist
 lend a hand to

J

WORD BANK: Jobs

Use words like these to tell about people's jobs.

bus driver	doctor	police officer
carpenter	firefighter	teacher
chef	nurse	

---

jump to spring into the air

Teeny and Tiny like to **jump**!
    hop
    leap

K

keep to put something in a safe or handy place

I **keep** my bones here.
 save
 store

My First Thesaurus

laugh to make sounds to show that something is funny
Bear's costume made her **laugh**.

chuckle
giggle
howl

little small in size or amount
Abby has a **little** house.

miniature
tiny
wee

look to see
We **look** at a big lion.

gaze
peek
stare

mad feeling and showing anger
Why does Hen seem so **mad**?

angry
bitter
cross

make to form, shape, or put together
Ben and Tim **make** a fort.

build
construct
create

near close to

Our house is **near** the beach.
> by
> next to

nice kind and thoughtful

Fran is a **nice** person.
> gentle
> good
> sweet

now at the present time

You must get on the bus **now**.
> at once
> immediately
> right away

pat to tap gently with an open hand

I love to **pat** the puppy.
> pet
> stroke

WORD BANK: People		
Use words like these to name people.		
aunt	child	mother
boy	father	sister
brother	girl	uncle

My First Thesaurus

WORD BANK: Places

Use words like these to name places.

city	mountain	school
country	ocean	store
house	park	zoo
lake		

pretty pleasing to the eye

These are such **pretty** flowers.

> beautiful
> lovely

put to move something to a certain spot

Put the dishes on the table.

Lay
Place
Set

quick very fast

Jill is **quick** at math.

> speedy
> swift

quiet with little or no noise

We were **quiet** in the library.

> hushed
> silent

rain to fall in drops of water from the clouds

It will **rain** soon.

> pour
> shower

ring a clear sound like that made by a bell

The loud **ring** woke up Yukio.

> clang
> gong
> jingle

run to move quickly on foot

They will **run** around the track.

> dash
> race
> sprint

---

sad with no happiness or joy

Penny Pig is **sad** about her hat.

> gloomy
> unhappy

My First Thesaurus

WORD BANK: Smell
Use these words to tell how something smells.

clean	fresh	stinky
fishy	salty	sweet
flowery	smoky	

said spoke aloud

Elli **said**, "I love my kitten."
- declared
- stated
- exclaimed

shine to give off light

The stars **shine** in the sky.
- glow
- sparkle
- twinkle

silly not serious

That is a very **silly** hat.
- amusing
- foolish
- funny

smart having a quick mind

Paula is **smart** in science.
- bright
- clever
- intelligent

WORD BANK: Sound

Use these words to tell how animals and things sound.

barking	noisy	soft
cackling	purring	squeaky
clanging	quacking	whistling
mooing		

stop to bring or come to a halt

When will the noise **stop**?
> cease
> end
> finish

strange not usual

His coat is **strange**.
> odd
> unusual
> weird

T

WORD BANK: Taste

Use these words to tell how something tastes.

bitter	sweet	sour
spicy	salty	yummy
fruity	tart	

---

trip a passing from one place to another

They took a **trip** across the sea.
> journey
> voyage

try to make an effort to do something

Anna will **try** to win the race.
> attempt
> strive

U

under lower than

The mouse is **under** the lion's paw.

　　below
　　beneath

upset sad or worried

Dad was **upset** when we were late.

　　disturbed
　　nervous

W

wash to clean using water and soap

It's time to **wash** the dog.

　　bathe
　　scrub

wet being covered with a liquid

The **wet** bathing suits must hang to dry.

　moist
　soaked

Y

yell to call out in a loud voice

The people at the game **yell**.

　　　scream
　　　holler
　　　shout

Index

Index

D

Dates
  in a letter, 84–85
  punctuating, 311–312,
    319, 321, 322, 329,
    336, H36
Definitions, dictionary,
  H9–H10, H11–H12
Descriptions
  using exact words, 270,
    271, 286, 287
  the writing process and,
    274–285
  See also Composition,
    types, descriptions
Details
  elaborating with, 12, 71,
    83, 84–85, 117, 139,
    143, 146, 149, 150,
    151, 157, 216, 218,
    219, 226–227,
    245–246, 270, 271,
    273, 275, 282, 287,
    H26
  listening for, 90–91
  organizing, 17
  recalling, 90–91
  using, 19, 21, 67, 74, 75,
    233
Dictionary, using a
  entry words, H7–H8
  definitions, H9–H10,
    H11–H12
  using, H15
Directions. *See* Instructions
Discussions
  how to conduct, 6, 7
  group, 6, 7
  about writing, 359
Drafting, 18–19, 74, 85,
    148, 157, 215, 225,
    232, 278, 287, 292,
    293, 351, 361, 367,
    H27

Drafts, revising
  for audience, 20–21, 293,
    367
  by combining, 99–100,
    171, 172, 220,
    251–252, 282, 356
  by deleting, 76
  by elaborating, 21, 67,
    71, 75, 82–83, 84–85,
    117, 139, 143, 146,
    149, 150, 151, 157,
    159, 215, 216, 217,
    218, 219, 224,
    226–227, 245–246,
    271, 273, 275, 279,
    281, 282, 286, 287,
    349, 351–352, 355,
    362–363, 365, 366,
    367, 368, H26
  for sentence fluency,
    35–36, 78, 99–100,
    109–110, 152,
    171–172
  for word choice, 76, 78,
    109–110, 117, 151,
    152, 185, 220, 253,
    280, 281, 282, 292,
    356
  See also Revising
Dramatic activities
  present interpretations,
    81, 155, 292

E

Editing. *See* Proofreading;
  Revising
Elaborating, 21, 67, 71, 75,
    82–83, 84–85, 117,
    139, 143, 146, 149,
    150, 151, 157, 159,
    215, 216, 217, 218,
    219, 224, 226–227,
    245–246, 271, 273,
    275, 279, 281, 282,
    286, 287, 345, 349,

    351–352, 355,
    362–363, 365, 366,
    367, 368, H26
Electronic catalog, H16
Encyclopedia, using, 229,
  H15, H16
End marks. *See* Exclamation
  points; Periods;
  Question marks
Ending, writing an, 149,
  209, 216, 217, 227,
  352, 353
Enrichment, 47, 118, 186,
  254, 319
Envelopes, addressing, 86
Evaluating
  meaning by interpreting
    visual images, 2, 8, 9,
    156, 160–161, 208,
    270, 286
  published models, 63–66,
    135–138, 207–208,
    267–270, 288–290,
    341–344
  student models, 68–69,
    84–87, 140–143,
    158–159, 210–211,
    226–227, 272–273,
    346–347, 362–363
  respond to others'
    writing, 76–77,
    150–151, 218–219,
    232–233, 280–281,
    292, 354, 367–368
  using criteria, 67, 75,
    139, 149, 209, 217,
    271, 279, 345, 353
Exact adjectives. *See*
  Adjectives, exact
Exact nouns. *See* Nouns,
  exact
Exact verbs. *See* Verbs,
  exact

Exclamation points, 45–46, 49, 50, 52, 61, 192, 307–308, 321, 326, 335, H37

Exclamations, 45–46, 49, 50, 52, 61, 192, 307–308, 321, 326, 335, H37

Expository composition. *See* Composition, modes

F

Fact and opinion, 230

Fiction, 102, 116, 135–138, 139, 140–143, 144–155, 156, 157, 168, 184, 304, H15

First draft, writing a, 12, 18–19, 68, 74, 85, 140–141, 148, 159, 215–217, 232, 278, 287, 292–293, 351–353, 361, 367, H27

G

Grammar glossary, H35–H39

Graphic organizers
character web, 146
describing wheel, H31
five "W's" chart, 71, 72, 73, H33
graphs, H17
idea tree, 291
idea wheel, H31
sequence charts, 17, 18, 19, 73, H34
spider map, H34
story map, 147, H33
tree chart, H32
word web, 16, 276, H32

Greeting, in letters, 84–87

Group discussions. *See* Discussions

H

Heading, in letters, 84–87

Helping verbs. *See* Verbs, helping

I

I, in compound subject, 111–112, 120, 121, 131, 194

Ideas, 9, 12, 14–17, 19, 70, 71, 73, 75, 144, 145, 146, 147, 212, 214, 216, 228, 271, 274, 275, 290, 348, 349, 350, 351, 352

Indenting, paragraphs, 18, 346

Information
listening for, 90–91

Informative writing. *See* Composition, modes, expository; Instructions; Research reports

Instructions
following, 235, 236–237
giving, 223, 234
sequence of, 208, 209, 210, 211, 217, 218, 219, 223, 224, 225, 234–235
writing, 6, 212–223, 224, 225

Internet, using, 50, 63, 69, 71, 73, 75, 79, 82, 83, 121, 135, 143, 145, 147, 149, 153, 156, 157, 158, 211, 214, 217, 221, 224, 225, 257, 273, 275, 276, 279, 283, 286, 287, 322, 341, 347, 349, 350, 353, 357, 360, 361, H24, H31

Interview, 318

Intonation, 4, 81, 155, 161, 223, 285, 294–295

Introduction, writing an, 19, 139, 148, 149, 209, 215, 217, 219, 226–227, 233, 271, 273, 278, 279, 281, 345, 351–352, 353

Invitations, 86–87

L

Language
adapting, 4, 5, 6, 7, 15, 17, 20, 21, 24–25, 67, 70, 71, 84–87, 88, 145, 146, 148, 149, 154, 155, 156, 209, 210, 211, 212, 216, 217, 218, 219, 222, 284, 285, 286, 293, 294–295, 345, 355, 358, 359, 362–363, 365, 366, 368, 369
choice, 4, 78, 109–110, 117, 151, 152, 185, 209, 220, 222, 253, 270, 271, 272, 280, 281, 282, 290, 291, 292, 293, 345, 353, 356
tone, 161

Legends, map, H18

Letters
activities for writing, 85–86, 176, 182, 306
parts of, 84–87
types of
friendly, 84–87, 306
invitation, 86–87
thank–you, 86–87, 182

Library, H15–H16

Index

Index

Index

Acknowledgments *continued*

"Mushrooms Are Umbrellas" by Arnold Spilka. Copyright ©1994 by Arnold Spilka. Used by permission of Marian Reiner for the author.

"My Glider" from A PIZZA THE SIZE OF THE SUN by Jack Prelutsky. Text copyright ©1996 by Jack Prelutsky. Used by permission of HarperCollins Publishers.

"Wind Song" from I FEEL THE SAME WAY by Lilian Moore. Copyright ©1967, 1995 by Lilian Moore. Used by permission of Marian Reiner for the author.

Book Report

I'M TOO BIG (JE SUIS TROP GROS) by Lone Morton, pictures by Steve Weatherill. Published 1994 by arrangement with Barron's Educational Series, Inc., Hauppauge, NY.

Student Handbook

Definitions of "chest," "fog," "mirror," "seed," "ship," "spot," "storm," "stripe" "subway," and "wing" from the HOUGHTON MIFFLIN PRIMARY DICTIONARY. Copyright ©1989 by Houghton Mifflin Company. Reproduced by permission from the HOUGHTON MIFFLIN PRIMARY DICTIONARY.

One Minute Warm-up

2/1 BEDTIME FOR FRANCES by Russell Hoban, pictures by Garth Williams, published by HarperCollins Publishers, 1960. Used by permission.

2/1 CLAP YOUR HANDS by Lorinda Byran Cauley, published by PaperStar Books, 1992. Used by permission.

2/1 GOLDILOCKS AND THE THREE BEARS retold and illustrated by James Marshall, published by Dial Books for Young Readers, 1988. Used by permission.

2/1 MR. PUTTER AND TABBY FLY THE PLANE by Cynthia Rylant, illustrated by Arthur Howard, published by Harcourt Brace & Company, 1997. Used by permission.

2/1 MRS. BROWN WENT TO TOWN by Wong Herbert Yee, published by Houghton Mifflin Company, 1996. Used by permission.

2/3 A BIRTHDAY BASKET FOR TÍA by Pat Mora, illustrated by Cecily Lang. Text copyright ©1992 by Pat Mora. Illustrations copyright ©1992 by Cecily Lang. Reprinted with the permission of Simon & Schuster Books for Young Readers, an imprint of Simon & Schuster Children's Publishing Division.

2/3 ABUELA by Arthur Dorros, illustrated by Elisa Kleven, published by Dutton Children's Books, 1991. Used by permission.

2/3 AUNT FLOSSIE'S HATS (AND CRAB CAKES LATER) by Elizabeth Fitzgerald Howard, paintings by James Ransome, published by Clarion Books, 1991. Used by permission.

2/3 CHILDREN AROUND THE WORLD by Lynda Snowdon, published by Macmillan Children's Books, 1982. Used by permission.

2/3 JULIUS by Angela Johnson, pictures by Dav Pilkey, published by Orchard Books, 1993. Used by permission.

2/3 HAPPY BIRTHDAY, DANNY AND THE DINOSAUR! story and pictures by Syd Hoff, published by HarperCollins Publishers, 1995. Used by permission.

2/5 MAC & MARIE & THE TRAIN TOSS SURPRISE by Elizabeth Fitzgerald Howard, illustrated Gail Gordon Carter. Illustration copyright©1993 by Gail Gordon Carter. Used with permission of the Author and BookStop Literary Agency. All rights reserved.

Acknowledgments *continued*

2/5 OLLY'S POLLIWOGS by Anne & Harlow Rockwell. Copyright ©1970 by Anne and Harlow Rockwell. First published by Doubleday & Co. Reprinted by permission of Curtis Brown Ltd.

2/5 THE SEASHORE BOOK by Charlotte Zolotow, paintings by Wendell Minor, published by HarperCollins Publishers, 1992. Used by permission.

2/7 NOW WE CAN HAVE A WEDDING! by Judy Cox, illustrated by DyAnne DiSalvo-Ryan, published by Holiday House, 1998. Used by permission.

2/9 A YEAR FOR KIKO by Ferida Wolff, illustrated by Joung Un Kim, published by Houghton Mifflin Company, 1997. Used by permission.

2/9 BABY RATTLESNAKE as told by Te Ata, adapted by Lynn Moroney, illustrated by Mira Reisberg. Story copyright ©1989 by Lynn Moroney. Pictures ©1989 by Mira Reisberg. Reprinted with permission of the publisher, Children's Book Press, San Francisco, CA.

2/9 MISS NELSON IS MISSING! by Harry Allard, illustrated by James Marshall, published by Houghton Mifflin Company, 1977. Used by permission.

2/9 ONE GIANT LEAP: THE STORY OF NEIL ARMSTRONG by Don Brown, published by Houghton Mifflin Company, 1998. Used by permission.

Student Writing Model Contributors

Celsey Bédard, Maurice Bonar, Christine Guzman, Matthew Hodges, Phillip A. Jackson, Candice Lubin, Sarah Rose Manning, Kelly O'Masta, Adam Pynn.

Credits

Illustrations

Andrea Arroyo: 49, 192, 240 (t), 241, 247 (t), 256, 320 **Bernard Adnet:** 33, 173 (t), 307 (t) **Christiane Beauregard:** 257, 288, 289, H5, H13 **Elizabeth Brandt:** 300 (bkgrd.) **Dan Brawner:** 95, 96 **Lizi Boyd:** 46, 240 (b), 248 (b) **Liz Callen:** 10, 47 (m & b), 50, 57, 148, 172, 184 (b), 195, 201, 213, 215 (b), 237, 239 (t), 249 (t), 291, 293, 319 (m), 331, 338, H3, H4, H6, H31 **John Cymerman:** 53, 54 Linda Davick: 47 (t), 186 (t), 254 (t), 319 (t), H7, H9, H10 **Chris Demarest:** 29 (t), 38 (t), 39, 58, 160, 168, 263, 314, 326, 329, 332 **Dorothy Donohue:** 31 (t), 177, 182 (t) **Daniel Dumont:** 316 **Tuko Fujisaki:** 55, 187, 321 **Lee Glynn:** 86, 87, 176 (b), 246, 298, 306 (bkgrd.), 313 (t), H17, H18 **Kristen Goeters:** 64-65, 66 **Myron Grossman:** 41, 181, 183, 215 (t), 299 (b), 307 (b), H11, H12 **Tim Haggerty:** 179, 200, 203, 297, 299 (t), 308 (t) **Jennifer Beck Harris:** 27, 43, 82, 95, 156, 166, 167 (b), 170, 174, 176 (t), 180, 182 (b), 184 (t), 224, 247 (b), 249 (b), 286, 304, 315 (b), 318, 360, H23 **Eileen Hine:** H45–H56 **John Hovell:** 32 (bkgrd.), 36, 38 (b), 42, 46 (bkgrd.), 59, 94 (b), 172 (bkgrd.), 208, 242 (b), 244 (b), 250 (bkgrd.), 252 (bkgrd.), 310, H21, H22, H27 **Benrei Huang:** 44 (t), 330 **Anne Kennedy:** 6, 12, 13, 15, 16, 19, 21, 23, 25, 67–70, 75–78, 80, 81, 83–86, 89, 91, 139–144, 146–150, 152–155, 157–159, 209–211, 214, 216–220, 222, 223, 225–232, 234, 235, 237, 271–274, 276, 279–282, 284, 285, 287, 290, 292, 295, 345–349, 351–359, 361–364, 366, 367, H20, H25, H26, H27, H28, H29, H30

Illustrations *continued*

Jared Lee: 261 **Andy Levine:** 29 (b), 37, 45 **Cynthia Malaran:** 254 (b), 255, 319 (b) **Claude Martinot:** 30 (t), 32 **Ferris Nicolais:** 302, 306, 312, 318 **Tim Nihoff:** 28, 40, 165, 193, 305, 309 (t), 315 (t) **Diane Paterson:** 72, 88, 90, 161, 167 (t), 186 (m), 194, 202, 204, 205, 220, 225, 233, 235, 262, 265, 327, 335, H15, H16 **Chris Reed:** 31 (b), 152, 185, 188, 234, 236, 242 (t), 264, 313 (b), 370, 371, H47–H56 **Tim Robinson:** 244 (t), 248 (t), 302 (bkgrd.), 316 (bkgrd.) **Ellen Sasaki:** 173 (b), 239 (b) **Michael Sloan:** 243, 249 (m) **Jackie Snider:** 30 (b), 34, 94 (t), 96, 337 **George Ulrich:** 277, 311 **Ted Williams:** 40 (bkgrd.), 44 (b); bkgrd. for: 68, 69, 74, 78, 79, 84, 140–143, 152, 153, 158, 164, 168, 170, 174, 178, 184, 185, 210, 211, 221, 226, 227, 231, 253, 272, 273, 282, 283, 308 (b), 312, 356, 357, 362.

Photographs

Cover Photograph: Douglas E. Walker/Masterfile

Fine Art: 82 National Museum of American Art, Washington, D.C./Art Resource **156** Peter Ralston/Charles Scribner's Sons **286** National Gallery, London, UK/The Bridgeman Art Library.

Getting Started: 1 (tl) Kit Kittle/Corbis **1** (tm) Lawrence Migdale/Mira **1** (tr) Ron Watts/Corbis **1** (bl) Lawrence Migdale/Mira **1** (bm) Photodisc **1** (br) Mark Tomalty/Masterfile **2–5, 7, 8, 14, 18, 20, 22, 24** Joel Benjamin **9** (tl) Don Stevenson/Mira **9 (tr)** Erika Stone/Mira **9** (bl & br) Lawrence Migdale/Mira **11** all images Photodisc. **Unit 1: 26** Daniel J. Cox/Tony Stone Images **30** Photodisc **35 (tl)** Tim Davis/Tony Stone Images **35 (tr)** Kennan Ward/Corbis **35** (bl) Tim Davis/Tony Stone Images **35** (br) Renée Lynn/Tony Stone Images **36** Norman Myers/Bruce Coleman, Inc. **39** Stephen Krasemann/Tony Stone Images **42** Robert Carr/Bruce Coleman, Inc. **48** Jeff Greenberg/Rainbow/PNI **56** Jim Cummins/FPG

60 Martin Rogers/Prism/FPG **61** Stephen Frisch/Stock-Boston. **Unit 2: 62** Alan Hicks/Tony Stone Images **71, 74, 77, 80, 81** Ken Karp. **Unit 3: 92** Ed Honowitz/Tony Stone Images **93** Harry DiOrio/The Image Works **99** Lawrence Migdale/Stock, Boston **100** Myrleen Ferguson/PhotoEdit **102** AJA Productions/Image Bank **103** (middle, l. to r.): Jose Carrillo/PhotoEdit, Arthur Tilley/FPG, Michael Newman/PhotoEdit, Bruce Byers/FPG, Barros & Barros/Image Bank, Stephen Simpson/FPG **103 (bottom, l. to r.):** Steve Skjold/PhotoEdit, Art Tilley/FPG, Lawrence Migdale/Stock Boston **105** Jeff Isaac Greenberg/Photo Researchers **106** Renée Lynn/Photo Researchers **111** Myrleen Ferguson/PhotoEdit **113** Myrleen Ferguson/PhotoEdit **114** (t) Hans Reinhard/Bruce Coleman, Inc. **114 (b)** Christine Steimer/OKAPIA/Photo Researchers, Inc. **115** Lawrence Migdale/Tony Stone Images **117 (l)** Alan & Sandy Carey/Photo Researchers, Inc. **117 (r) R.** Hutchings/PhotoEdit **118** Donna Day/Tony Stone Images **120** Michael Newman/PhotoEdit. **Unit 4: 134** Ron Chapple/FPG **145, 146, 147, 151, 155** Ken Karp. **Unit 5: 162** Chip Simons/FPG **163** Bill Bachman/Photo Researches, Inc. **164** William Whitehurst/The Stock Market **164 (tl & tr)** William Whitehurst/The Stock Market **164 (l)** Keith Gunnar/Bruce Coleman **164 (r)** Martin Rogers/Tony Stone Images **165** Bob Daemmrich/ The Image Works **169** Robin Smith/ **170** Chip Simons/FPG **171** Stephen Simpson/FPG **174** Lawrence Migdale/Photo Researchers, Inc. **175** Jeanne Drake/ Tony Stone Images **177** Tom Prettyman/ Photo Edit **178** Margaret Miller/Photo Researchers, Inc. **179** Michael Newman/Photo Edit **185** Hans Reinhard/Bruce Coleman, Inc. **186** Turner & Devries/Image Bank **189** Chuck Place/Stock Boston **196** Alan Hicks/Tony Stone Images **197** Gary A. Conner/PhotoEdit **198** Frank Fournier/The Stock Market

Photographs *continued*

199 Tom Stewart/The Stock Market. **Unit 6: 206** G. & V. Chapman/The Image Bank **212, 216, 219, 223, 228, 230, 233** Ken Karp **231** Buddy Mays/Corbis. **Unit 7: 238** Index Stock Imagery **241** Adamsmith Productions/Corbis **243** James L. Amos/Corbis **245 (l)** Tetsu Yamazaki/International Stock **245 (m)** Patrice Ceisel/Stock Boston **245 (r)** Sunstar/International Stock **250 C.** Carton/Bruce Coleman, Inc. **251 (t)** E.R. Degginger/Photo Researchers **251 (r)** Nikolas Konstantinou/Tony Stone Images **251 (l)** Andrew Wood/Photo Researchers **252 M**. Kahl/Photo Researchers **253 (l)** Robert Brenner/PhotoEdit **253 (r)** Robert Brenner/PhotoEdit **254** Tom Young/The Stock Market. **Unit 8: 266** Douglas E. Walker/Masterfile **275, 278, 281, 284, 285, 292, 294** Ken Karp. **Unit 9: 296** Ariel Skelley/The Stock Market **297** Jonathan Nourok/PhotoEdit **300** Tom Hussey/Image Bank **301** Myrleen Ferguson/PhotoEdit **302** Russell D. Curtis/Bruce Coleman, Inc. **303** Richard Price/FPG **304** Michael Heron/Stock Market **305** Merritt Vincent/PhotoEdit **317** Art Wolfe/Tony Stone Images **328** David Young-Wolff/PhotoEdit/PNI **333** Dan Tardif/The Stock Market **334** Ariel Skelley/The Stock Market **336** Ken Chernus/FPG **339** Douglas Faulkner/The Stock Market. **Unit 10: 340** Stuart Westmorland/Tony Stone Images **341, 342-343** Suki Coughlin **344** Mario D. Mercado **348, 350, 352, 354, 355, 356, 358, 359, 364, 368, 369** Ken Karp **363** Photodisc.